Norman Jacobs

COLCHESTER

The Last Hundred Years

To John
(Happy Birthday at last!)
Norman Jacobs

Tyndale + Panda Publishing

First published 1989 by Tyndale + Panda Publishing Ltd.
117 High Street, Lowestoft, Suffolk.

Printed in England by Tyndale Press (Lowestoft) Ltd.,
Wollaston Road, Lowestoft, Suffolk.

ISBN 1 870094 07 7

Acknowledgements

I am extremely grateful to the many people who have willingly given up hours of their time to help me with this book. There are so many that I could not possibly acknowledge them all without running into a second volume! To those I haven't got room to mention, my apologies and grateful thanks.

Firstly, I must thank those "old" (in age but not in spirit) Colcestrians who let me into their memories and told me about the Colchester of days gone by. In particular I should like to thank Mr. Jack Gomer, Mr. & Mrs. Wally Lawrence and Mr. Bill Dent. I am also extremely grateful to Mr. Rod Pawsey of the Colchester Dock Transit Co.; Mr. Clifford Pawsey of Cant's Roses, Mr. Wollard-Shore, formerly of Colchester Royal Grammar School (now at Colne High School, Brightlingsea), Mr. Brook of Colchester Oyster Fishery Ltd., Mrs. V. A. Last of St. John's Green Primary School, Mr. David Forder of the *Mercury Theatre*, Messrs R. N. Collins & W. Breedon of Colchester Borough Transport, Mr. M. K. Holden of Eastern National, Mr. Don Reid of Colchester Rugby Club, Mr. Hal Mason of Colchester Football Club, Mr. Paul Bookbinder of Marks & Spencer, Mr. Andrew Phillips and Mr. Glen Jackson, all of whom gave up a good chunk of their busy time to see me.

I also received a great deal of help from a number of people I never actually met but whose correspondence was the source of much information: Bridget Williams of J. Sainsbury & Co., Mr. I. M. Denison of Colchester Lathe Co. and Mr. R. Rouse of Paxman's.

A number of local shops also responded enthusiastically to my enquiries, including Hatfield's of Colchester, Cullingford's, Lay & Wheeler and Kent, Blaxill.

The Essex County Library Service were also most helpful, in particular I must mention Mr. Frank Black at Clacton and Mr. Richard Shackle at Colchester.

Thanks also to Sandra Mooney for her help with the typing and to the rest of the 7:11 from Thorpe regulars — Cilla, Alan, Bill, Richard and even Brenda — for continually encouraging me to get on with the book.

I owe an extra special debt of gratitude to Mrs. Barbara Winter, without whose expert and painstaking help and advice with the photographs this book might have been all text!

And finally to all three generations of my immediate family for having had to live with my obsession with Colchester — thank you!

Ownership of individual photogrphs and post cards is acknowledged elsewhere. Where there is no acknowledgement the item comes from the author's own collection.

Norman Jacobs
Clacton-on-Sea
May 1989

Photo Credits

The author is most grateful to the following who have kindly lent photographs:

Mr. G. Jackson (page) 9, 12, 17, 38, 84, 87, 99 (top); *Mrs. D. Johnson* 10; *Mr. A. Phillips* 11, 31 (top), 45, 46, 67, 100 (top); *Mr. T. B. K. Davies* 21 (bottom), 35, 40, 56; *Colchester Royal Grammar School* 22, 109, 110, 111; *Colchester Lathe Co.,* 24, 60, 88 (top); *Marks & Spencer plc* 27, 50, 51, 52; *Woolworths plc* 28, 54, 55; *Mr. I. Jacobs* 31 (bottom), 95; *Mr. and Mrs. J. Gomer* 38 (top), 74; *J. Sainsbury's Archives* 42, 48, 49; *Colchester Oyster Fishery Ltd.* 62; *Mr. T. Griddle* 76; *Eastern National* 78; *Mr. R. N. Collins* 79; *Mrs. D. French* 85 (top), 100 (bottom); *Mercury Theatre* 88 (bottom); *Mr. W. Lawrence* 90; *Mr. W. Dent* 94; *Mrs. F. A. Johnson* 104 (bottom); *University of Essex* 106.

Contents

For Mum and Dad

One Hundred Years Ago

''Well I am glad to hear that something has moved the old town at last.''
— The Rev. C. H. Spurgeon, on hearing the news of the 1884 Colchester Earthquake.

Colchester approached the 1880s as a largely agricultural centre with some new industrial developments. Just ten years later, Colchester had become a modern industrial town with agriculture playing only a subsidiary role in its economy.

At the start of the decade the local newspaper headlines were grabbed by the furious debate going on at the Colchester Corn Market between those who wished to introduce the ''cental'' and those who opposed this new-fangled measure. The cental was a measure of weight equivalent to 100lbs. What had occasioned the row was a notice put up at Colchester Corn Market stating ''After 1st January 1880 Wheat will be purchased by the Cental. It is hoped that all will facilitate this change to a simpler mode of doing business which has worked satisfactorily on other markets.''

However, in a debate held in the town, Mr. W. S. Richardson of Layer Breton spoke for all the local farmers when he said he was ''strongly opposed to selling wheat by weight — it would occasion them a great deal of trouble and inconvenience without doing them any good whatever.'' The debate raged on over several pages of Colchester's very first newspaper of the 1880s — The *Essex Standard* dated January 3rd, 1880 — with the millers and merchants strongly in favour of the change and the farmers and corn growers equally vehemently opposed.

National news at the time included a report of the Tay Bridge disaster and a dispatch from one of the far-flung reaches of the Empire commending Lord Roberts for his ''speedy dispersion'' of 10,000 Afghans. The *Standard's* comment on this was that ''we should . . . neither be alarmed nor surprised when we are called upon to defend the Empire which has been confined to our care.'' (By whom was not stated!)

Another interesting editorial comment referred to a speech made by Gladstone, who had attacked the Government of Lord Beaconsfield. ''Gladstone is now making a great noise,'' thundered the Conservative *Essex Standard*, ''but fifty years hence the name of Lord Beaconsfield will be mentioned a hundred times for one that his is thought of.'' (Oh well, you can't win them all . . .)

Meanwhile, back in Colchester, the Town Council had placed an advertisement in that same paper: ''Purchase of Water Works — Loan of £100,000 required by order, Henry Jones, Town Clerk.'' The advert went on to explain that the loan was to ''provide the purchase money payable by the council on their acquiring the undertaking of the Colchester Water Works Company and for extending their Works and the Supply of Water and will be required by the 25th day of March next.''

The money was raised in time and in October 1880, at a formal ceremony at the bottom of Balkerne Hill, Peter Bruff, the private owner of the waterworks, handed over his works, his premises and his five employees to the Colchester Corporation.

The water supply in Colchester had been a long running political, social and economic battle. The taking into public-ownership of this vital public utility marked the beginning of a new era, though not quite the end of the battle.

The next step was to build a new water-tower to improve the supply. The decision to do this was taken in August 1881 and tenders for the new tower and water tank were sought. Both were eventually let to local firms — the tank and ironwork contract went to Arthur Mumford of the Culver Street Ironworks (though in the event he had to sub-contract to a firm in Newcastle) and the brick tower to Henry Everett and Son of Hythe Hill.

Not everyone was happy about this decision to build a new water tower. The Conservative opposition on the council in particular felt that the ruling Liberal group were merely wasting ratepayers money and that the whole venture was a mistake. They were concerned that the inhabitants of the more rural parts of the borough, Mile End and Lexden for example (mostly Conservative supporters), would be forced to pay higher rates whilst receiving no benefit at all from the new tower.

To one man, the Rev. John Irvine, Rector of St. Mary's-at-the-Walls, however, the opposition became a very personal matter when he discovered that the new water-tower was to be built only sixteen feet away from his back door and that, eighty-five feet above his head, a cast iron tank would be holding 230,000 gallons — or approximately 1000 tons of water. Having got nowhere by taking the matter up directly with the Council, the Rev. Irvine wrote an historic letter to the *Essex Standard.* In it he referred to the Water Tower as 'Jumbo', a name which has stuck ever since.

In the end, in spite of all the opposition, 'Jumbo' was finally built and officially opened by the Mayor, John Bawtree Harvey, on September 27th, 1883. Most of the Conservative opposition stayed away. The concern which John Irvine and many others had expressed about the safety of such a structure was soon to be put to a very severe test. At 9.18 on the morning of April 22nd, 1884, just seven months after that official opening, an Earthquake struck Colchester and all the neighbouring villages and countryside. The *Essex Chronicle* of April 25th, 1884 reported that altogether there were four shocks and that ''every building in the town was shaken.'' School children ran shrieking from their schools, workmen rushed out of their workplaces and women fainted in the streets. Many buildings were severely damaged.

Amongst the worst hit was Lion Walk Congregational Church, whose spire was brought crashing to the ground, amid dark mutterings from the more fundamental Congregationalists that it was a sign from God on the offensive nature of such an elaborate building. St. Nicholas's Church Tower was cracked; the roof of the Wesleyan Day School in Culver Street was split; the chimneys at

''Jumbo'' — symbol of the brave new world of the 1880s — named by Rev. John Irvine after the famous elephant sold to Barnham's circus by London Zoo. Because of the fuss created by Irvine the water tank was initially only half filled. John Irvine's memory is perpetuated by the road named after him.

Hythe Station were destroyed; many houses in North Hill lost their chimneys as they did in both Long and Short Wyre Streets. In Maidenburgh Street an old house was almost demolished and practically all the houses and shops in Head Street, Hight Street, Magdalen Street, Barrack Street and Hythe Hill suffered considerable damage. Scarcely a house was left intact in Brook Street and East Hill. Even at Lexden two houses lost their roofs. Altogether the cost of the damage was put at as much as £200,000.

Oh yes, the Water Tower, the subject of so much concern? The *Essex Chronicle* had this to say: ''The high Water Tower remains intact, and has not sustained the slightest damage.''

Perhaps C. H. Spurgeon was right and that the earthquake did move the old town, but it also had a big push from the up-and-coming generation of entrepreneurs — James Paxman, Joseph Blomfield, Wilson Marriage, John Kavanagh and many others. Industrialisation speeded up throughout the 1880s, new factories were built and existing ones expanded. The population grew from 28,374 in 1881 to 34,559 in 1891. Building spread out towards Lexden and the other suburbs. Electricity came to Colchester in the 1880s when a private company opened a plant in Culver Street. There was even talk of electric trams in 1887, though at the time the plans came to nothing.

At the same time as the town was beginning to expand a Colchester magistrate was able to say ''Corn growing is undoubtedly doomed in Essex . . . to continue it means ruin to landowners, farmers and labourers alike.'' In 1882 Severalls Farm was worth just one shilling an acre.

The bustling town of Colchester that we know today came to life just about 100 years ago. The 1880s may have begun with a last desperate attempt to cling to the past with a futile and increasingly anachronistic argument about the cental, but it finished with Colchester firmly facing the future as a modern industrial town. And somehow 'Jumbo' symbolised the whole process — the one large structure to be unaffected by the Earthquake — the result of modern thinking, modern building and modern engineering. Even today, Jumbo stands watching over the town as a reminder of the decade when Colchester shook off the old ways and welcomed the new.

Town Hall. The Insubstantial Town Hall built in 1844 on the site of the old Norman Moot Hall. It lasted little more than fifty years before being swept aside in Colchester's confident revolution of the late Victorian period.

◀ An 1880s view of the High Street showing the impressive Essex and Suffolk Fire Office originally built in 1820 as a Corn Exchange, on the ground floor, with the Insurance Company's office upstairs. It has served many different purposes in its 160-odd years but the name 'Fire Office' seems to have stuck.

The 1887 Golden Jubilee celebrations outside the Fire Office. The Fire Engine was still in the private hands of the Essex & Suffolk Insurance Company. (But they did promise to put out anyone's fire even if they weren't insured with them!)

Late Victorian and Edwardian Colchester

The process begun in the 1880s continued unabated throughout the 1890s and the early years of the twentieth century. By the 1911 census only 838 men gave their occupation as having anything to do with farming or market gardening, whereas over 5000 were working in the factories, building trade or transport. Trades Unions boomed between 1890 and 1914 and until the outbreak of the First World War wages continued to rise steadily.

The Corporation had continued the process, begun with the waterworks, of providing amenities for all — electricity followed in 1898 and an electric tram service in 1904. The local authorities at both borough and county level were actively involved in providing schools, parks, swimming facilities and a library.

The High Street was flourishing as a shopping centre worthy of such a modern town. Some of the big High Street names were beginning to open up in Colchester, Sainsbury's, Boots, Marks & Spencer's. Culver Street was becoming a thriving industrial street. Housing was continuing to push onwards and outwards — new estates were built, such as New Town and Creffield. This was the period when the *Hippodrome* Music Hall was flourishing as well as the *Theatre Royal;* when young men met their young ladies at *The Top of the Town* or, if you were 'posh', you took a promenade on Saturday nights down Lexden Road. You could get a meal at Aberdein's in Long Wyre Street for ninepence or buy a suit at Clamp's Stores in St. Botolph's Street for ten shillings and elevenpence. At Harris Bros in Long Wyre Street you could get tea for one-and-sixpence a pound. The Head Post Office was open from 7.00a.m. to 10.00p.m. on weekdays and from 7.00a.m. to 10.00a.m. and 5.00p.m. to 6.00p.m. on Sundays. And in 1894, the first telephone exchange was opened for twenty-nine subscribers.

The population rose from 34,559 in 1891 to 43,452 in 1911. And through it all Colchester exuded confidence. Everything was done on a grand scale. For Queen Victoria's Diamond Jubilee of 1897 the Council laid on a spectacular day's celebrations including a cycling carnival, a battle of flowers, a procession led by the Standard Ironworks Band and, to top it off, a free *fête* on Abbey Fields (attended by 20,000 people), with fireworks and a bonfire in the evening.

In 1906, the General Election was fought out in electric lights with the Liberals proclaiming ''Pearson suits Colchester'' outside the Cups Hotel, while the Conservatives fought back with ''Keep Evans on Top''.

In 1909 the magnificent Colchester Pageant was held.

And symbolising it all, in 1902, the new Town Hall was built as a monument to the civic pride and confidence now coursing through the veins of Colcestrians. Designed, in response to a public competition, by Sir John Belcher, it took some three years to build at a cost of around £50,000, with the fine Victoria Tower being entirely paid for by Alderman James Paxman out of his own pocket. The new Town Hall swept the old faltering, insubstantial building of 1844 into oblivion. Wilson Marriage and Gurney Benham wrote that Colchester Town Hall should be a ''model building of its kind'' and ''an unfailing source of attraction and interest''.

Like Jumbo, Colchester Town Hall has also stood the test of time and still stands as a living monument to that proud period of Colchester's history when peace, confidence, prosperity and growth went forward hand in hand ready to meet the challenges thrown up by the twentieth century.

The High Street looking towards St. Nicholas Church in the Edwardian period. This particular building had a relatively short life span as churches go, lasting from 1876 until it was demolished in 1955. Part of the churchyard still survives as a garden behind the Co-operative department store, which now occupies the site. The tower and spire were taken down 'brick-by-brick' and re-errected in America.

The new Town Hall built by John Belcher earned Colchester the nickname 'Belchester' (Beautiful Town in French). This photograph must have been taken shortly after it was opened in 1902 as the tram lines — laid down in 1904 — are conspicuous by their absence.

North Hill sometime after 1904 showing the rapidly changing face of travel technology with a horse and cart, a tram and a motor car. Simkin's the Furniture Dealer was one of Colchester's long-lived businesses, lasting from about 1880 until well after the Second World War.

St. Botolph's Street about 1910 with Griffin's furniture depository on the left. Many of the buildings in St. Botolph'a Street were destroyed in 1944 in Colchester's worst air-raid of the Second World War when fire-bombs rained down upon the area.
The road on the left is Osborne Street next to which was situated Smiths the greengrocers; Hancocks, who were confectioners; Allens, the butchers and Sturgeons, ironmongers.

Long Wyre Street just before the First World War with Boots on the right hand corner. Boots was one of the first national shops to arrive in Colchester, having opened at the turn of the century. On the left of the photograph is Pages who were gent's outfitters.

High Street in the late 1930s with the Fire Office still as dominating as ever.

The High Street before the days of shopping precincts when shops such as Woolworths, Hiltons and Babyland made it the shopping centre.

The Nineteen-Twenties and Thirties

The last great revival of the Victorian and Edwardian confidence came with the unveiling and dedication of the War Memorial on May 24th, 1923. Originally intended to be just the monument designed by H. C. Fehr, the whole thing took on a much more significant importance when Viscount Cowdray, formerly Sir Weetman Pearson, MP for Colchester, bought both the Castle and Hollytrees to present to the town, so that the monument became just the centrepiece of a much larger memorial.

It was on Empire Day 1923 that Alderman Wilson Marriage asked the Rt. Hon. Viscount Cowdray, P.C. (High Steward of Colchester) to "accept the Gift of a Golden Key and unlock the Gates and declare the New Entrance and Extension open to the public." The mayor then accepted the gifts on behalf of the Borough and the monument, set in the magnificent sweep of Cowdray Crescent, was unveiled.

Colchester grew much more slowly between the wars and change was more gradual. It was a preiod for consolidation following the hectic growth from 1880 – 1914. However, the demolition of houses to make way for the War Memorial had highlighted the fact that there was now a serious shortage of housing in the town. In an effort to combat this, the Council built a number of housing estates at Mile End, at Lexden, off the Harwich Road and at Old Heath. The first eighteen council houses in Colchester were built in Defoe Crescent at a cost of £1,200. Rent and rates for a three bedroom house came to sixteen shillings and ninepence per week. Together with the increase in private house building it led to many of the old suburbs and out-lying villages becoming submerged into Colchester itself - areas such as Old Heath, Shrub End, Mile End and Lexden.

Many of the new houses in the Barrack Street area cost just over £300 in 1930. A deposit of £100 and a mortgage of £200 would have cost something like twenty-eight shillings a month.

During this period the town was still seen by those who lived in it as a friendly place where everyone knew their neighbours, where you could leave your front door open and where the children could play in the street without having to worry too much about motor cars. Where, on a Saturday, those same youngsters could go to the Cattle Market and see the ponies being driven from the Railway Station to be sold for two or three guineas each before going on to see Tom Mix and his horse Tony at the 'pictures' and buying a pie from Mrs McCluskey's in

Butt Road. Where on a Sunday they would 'bunk-out' of Sunday School to go and see the band playing in Castle Park.

But changes were already beginning to take place. In 1926 a coach and omnibus park was opened in St. John's Street and in 1928 the Corporation began replacing its tram fleet with motor buses. Trips to the coast were becoming more and more the norm and, particularly with the ever-increasing popularity of Clacton-on-Sea, the town centre became choked up on Saturdays and Sundays. The Summer of 1933 proved to be a sign of things to come for Colchester when the Northern by-pass between Lexden and Greenstead was opened. (Incidentally, as a side consequence of this, many of the locals forsook their Lexden Road promenade on Sunday evenings in favour of the new leisure-time activity of viewing the stationary lines of traffic returning — or trying to return — from the coast).

Things were also changing slowly in the town centre. More 'London' shops were starting to open up in Colchester, though, in the main, it was still a period when owner-occupiers lived over their shops and took a pride in being polite and courteous to their customers. There was also less encroaching on each other's business. Shopping in general was less hurried and the pace of everything stll much slower than today. As one octogenerian Colcestrian, Jack Gomer, told me "It's all such a rush now. You have to get your own things and then queue up to pay. I call it a damn sauce! There is nothing so nice as being looked after in shops." He also told me that he could remember when Reckitt's Blue only cost an old penny — "It's 43p now . . . and smaller!" Industry was gradually moving away from the Town Centre, Mumford's being the last to go in 1933.

On Saturday mornings the High Street would be chock-a-block full of people visiting the market looking for bargains and with trams still rattling along the street and later buses it is surprising that there were not many serious accidents or that people were able to get around at all. There was a special problem near the Town Hall where one small area between the tram tracks and the pavement was designated as the starting point for all buses leaving Colchester. There were shoppers, bus passengers, tram passengers, cinema queues (outside the *Hippodrome*) and street traders all mixed together. And, as if that wasn't bad enough, this small section of the High Street also contained the Silver Queen bus depot, a taxi-rank and the entrance to the public conveniences!

Municipal enterprise was still there but had slowed down and consisted mainly of consolidating what it already had. The Corporation built a new generating station for its electricity supply in 1927 on Hythe Quay; it fought off a proposal from Eastern National to run its buses and, when Mumford's closed, it decided to build a new public library on the site. Though, in the event, the Library was never fully completed as part of the site was eventually devoted to a car park. The bricks for the unfinished portion of the Library lay unused in a field where they remained until they were finally sold off in the 1960s.

A bit of rural tranquility. Abbott's Road, Old Heath, in its ember days as an outlying village in the 1920s. On the right is the old Saint Barnabas Church, destroyed by fire in the early 1950s. ▶

Head Street in the late 1930s. The building on the right of the present Post Office was the first Post Office built in 1874.

As the '20s and 30s approached their end, a new atmosphere crept over Colchester. War was in the air and in September 1938, gangs of labourers began digging trenches on the Recreation Ground, St John's Green and the Hollytrees Meadow. At the same time the WVS started and in August 1939 shopkeepers filled their newly-arrived sandbags. It was the beginning of a new era for Colchester.

So far we have taken Jumbo and the New Town Hall as our symbols of the different periods. It would be nice to take the Castle and Hollytrees as the symbol of the '20s and '30s, but perhaps, with the benefit of hindsight, it may be more appropriate as a sign of things to come to take the by-pass . . .

A peaceful Sheepen Bridge in 1926 built on the site of the ford across the river. This formed part of a track which led from the old cattle market at the bottom of North Hill along Sheepen Road, across the river and on to West Bergholt.

Colchester Since The War

Once the war came to an end in 1945 normal life returned to Colchester at much the same pace as the 1920s and '30s. The bomb damage incurred brought no major problems, but once again the problem of a shortage of housing arose. Old Council housing estates were enlarged and new ones built at Barn Hall Estate, Monkwick and Shrub End. The population in 1951 was 57,449 (compared to 43,393 in 1921).

Life in Colchester from 1945 to the late 1960s continued on its peaceful way with perhaps just one rude shock to its system on the night of 31st January, 1953. This was the night of the Great East Coast Floods which devastated coastal towns all along the east coast of Britain. In particular low lying areas such as Jaywick Sands and Canvey Island suffered severe damage to property and much loss of life — 35 people died in Jaywick on that night.

Colchester experienced nothing as bad as this but nevertheless the area around the Hythe was inundated and most of the factories had to close for a day or two as water three or four feet deep covered their floors.

The worst affected road was Hawkins Road with water completely flooding the ground floors of the houses while families had to watch helplessly as their furniture and personal belongings were ruined by a great rush of salt water. Only the tops of the lamp posts were visible as the road was virtually turned into a canal. The local farmers also suffered and 177 sheep were drowned when Horsey Island was flooded.

A flood relief fund was set up by the Mayor with a target of £1,000. In just two weeks the total reached was £3,018.

Although the population of Colchester continued to grow throughout the '50s and '60s (accelerated by the coming of Essex University and the electrification of the railway line to London) it was still easily recognisable as the town that had served its people well since the 1880s. Memories of even the mid-1960s recall the town as a peaceful one and bring back recollections of Saturday morning loitering at the Cattle Market — still as popular as it had been in the 1920s.

The early 1960s had seen the first hint of what was to come when the market was moved from the High Street to Culver Street, though, in the end, it had to be moved back again. But by the end of the decade the town planners had decided that something had to be done about the ever-increasing number of people shopping in the town centre together with the ever-increasing volume of cars. And so the era of shopping precincts, multi-story car parks and ring roads was born.

◀ The Colchester Lathe Co.'s rowing boat being put to good use during the 1953 floods at the Hythe. It is shown here taking salvage workers into the factory where, two days after the flood, there was still over four feet of flood water.

The ever-present Fire Office in a 1950s view of the High Street.

◀ The area around the Hythe as it looked the day after the floods came. The building, top right, was the old gas works and those on the left, Spottiswood Ballantyne's printing works.

The first steps were taken with the planning of the Lion Walk shopping precinct between 1968 and 1970. Eventually finished at the end of 1975, it completely changed the character of Colchester. It chopped the ancient town centre thoroughfare of Culver Street in two and increased the number of chain stores in the town, while at the same time causing great alarm to the High Street shopkeepers who saw all their trade heading for the new ''shoppers paradise''.

The precinct was followed by the birth of a number of multi-story car parks at Middleborough, Queen Street, St. John's Street and St. Mary's, all of which did their bit to change Colchester irrevocably. The motor car also dictated the wholesale demolition of areas of land to the south of the town centre, including practically everything within sight at St. Botolph's Corner! This was to make way for the Southway dual carriageway from the Mersea Road to the Maldon Road. Though, in fact, even this had its brighter aspect for, in spite of tearing up the southern part of the town, it had the effect of 'saving' St. John's Street as there was a dramatic reduction in the number of vehicles using this road with a consequence that the street became environmentally more attractive for pedestrians.

The latest in the long line of recent developments is the Culver Street precinct complete with ornamental fountain and yet more big stores in Debenham's and C & A's.

In 1981, the *Essex County Standard* said that ''Colchester continues to remain a vigorous and bustling centre. It may not be the cosy market town that it was only 20 years ago, but it still retains enough charm and individuality to make it popular with residents and visitors''.

The Symbol for post-war Colchester? Perhaps the next 100 years — here's to them!

Culver Street as it looked in 1962. Still one street with some of the town's oldest shops, a modest car park (definately not multi-story!) and not a shopping precinct in sight.

◀ St. John's Street before the advent of Tesco's but after the coming of the NAAFI Club, with the *Playhouse* still open for business as a cinema further up the street. Bus station on left behind Cook's butcher shop.

Hard to believe that this view of Culver Street is just twenty years old, having been taken in the late 1960s. This part of the street has now disappeared altogether and has been incorporated into the Lion Walk Shopping Precinct. The Woolworth's building and Beaumont's the Hairdresser are now occupied by Dixons, Miss Selfridge and Exchange Travel while the house in the background has now become John Hillary Travel.

Military and Wartime

Colchester probably owes its very existence to the fact that it is a strategic military site. The Iron Age tribe, the Trinovantes, who first settled here were attracted by a ridge of gravel that not only commanded the nearby countryside but also supplied pure water and, though itself free of woodland, was surrounded by thick forest.

When the Belgae, pushing northwards and eastwards from roughly what is now Kent and Hertfordshire reached Essex, they attacked the Trinovantes and defeated them, killing their king. His son, Mandubracius, fled to Rome and called on Julius Caesar for assistance. Caesar returned with him and, in turn, defeated the Belgae, by now known as the Catuvellauni, and restored Mandubracius. More battles were to follow between the warring tribes until the Belgic Cunobelin appeared on the scene and took over the Trinovantean territory setting up his capital on that same gravel ridge, calling it Camulodunum. By the time of the Roman invasion in AD43, Camulodunum, because of its fine defensive position, had become capital of most of south-east Britain. This made it an obvious target for the Romans who eventually conquered it and probably set up a small fortress. The town then became, under the Romans, Colonia Claudia Victrencensis, a colony of veteran soldiers.

Colchester's next great battle came when Boudicca, Queen of the Iceni, linked up with the Trinovantes and laid the town waste. After she had eventually been defeated the Romans rebuilt Colchester with a wall, ditch and rampart. Much of the wall is in evidence today and, in general, still forms the boundary for Colchester town centre.

More battles followed, with first the Saxons attacking the town and then the Danes. When the Normans arrived they too recognised the importance of Colchester and erected, about 1090, a castle keep half as large again as the 'White' Tower of London.

Colchester then saw action in 1216, when a detachment of French soldiers sent to aid the Barons in their struggle against King John, garrisoned the Castle and were besieged by Savaric the Bloody. Eventually the French surrendered.

Colchester's next great military adventure came in 1648 with the Siege of Colchester. Throughout the Civil War, Colchester had remained a staunchly Parliament town, but a Royalist force under Sir Charles Lucas and Sir George Lisle seized the town on June 12th, 1648 and turned it into a Royalist Garrison. When the Parliamentary army under Fairfax caught up with it they immediately attacked and a raging battle was fought at Head Gate. By the end of the day,

The Siege House by East Bridge, scene of some fierce fighting during the Civil War. The timbers are still to this day pock-marked with holes made by Royalist bullets fired during the Siege. Now a restaurant.

Fairfax was forced to withdraw and set up camp on Lexden Heath. Colchester was now under siege.

Fairfax encircled the town and another fierce skirmish took place on St. John's Green. By 27th August it was clear that the defenders had no hope and they surrendered. Lucas and Lisle were executed and the town ordered to pay compensation which, considering the townspeople were actually on Parliament's side, seems a bit harsh.

Because of its position on the main road from London to Harwich, Colchester became a centre for troop assemblies and there was much grumbling in the town over billeting arrangements. In 1793, the innkeepers petitioned the Corporation to encourage the Government to build a barracks in the town. The petition had its effect and in 1796 the North Devonshire Regiment marched in to the newly built barracks on land to the south-east of the town. An area commemorated today in names such as Barrack Street and Artillery Street.

By 1803 the barracks could accommodate 700 cavalry and 6,000 infantry. In October of that year, the local commander warned the townspeople that invasion by Napoleon was imminent and placed a Captain's Guard in the High Street. Many of the leading Colchester families fled inland. Needless to say the invasion never came.

Part of the old Napoleonic period barracks in Barrack Street. This was the last remaining section and did not disappear until 1927.

One of the first German soldiers, in the new barracks, which returned to Colchester after the Crimean War. Photographed by J. Schofield of Mersea Road, one of Colchester's leading photographers in the Victorian and Edwardian period.

Following the defeat of Napoleon at Waterloo in 1815, the authorities considered that there was no longer any need to maintain the barracks at Colchester. Consequently, in October 1816, they were put up for sale by public auction. Troops were once more billeted around the town and once again the local innkeepers complained. But it was to be the Crimean War that was to lead to barracks returning to Colchester. This war had exposed the lack of proper accommodation for the soldiers and so it was that in 1856, the North Devonshire Regiment once again became the first troops to march into Colchester to occupy the new barracks.

At first the barracks consisted of wooden huts, but gradually they were replaced by brick buildings — the Meanee and Hyderabad barracks being built in 1891, while the Sobraon and Goojerat barracks as well as the Military Hospital were built during the Boer War.

Colchester's first contingent of troops for the Boer War, the 6th Company of the Army Service Corps, left on October 11th, 1899. A couple of evenings prior to departure they attended the *Theatre Royal* to see *The Death-or-Glory-Boys!* On the morning of their embarkation they were each provided with a free tin of tobacco by Mr. O. J. Durrant of Head Street.

As the troops became a permanent fixture, so they became more involved in the social life of the town and were invited to civic functions and gala nights at the theatres where the dress uniforms of the officers livened up the drab black of the civilians' formal attire. They, in their turn, repayed the compliment by giving dances and providing regimental bands for special occasions.

The contribution the soldiers made to the local tradesmen's profits was tempered only by their sometimes over-enthusiastic behaviour in the town. But gradually, although the colourful uniforms eventually gave way to dull khaki, the garrison became fully integrated into the life and prosperity of the town. The Tattoo is an annual reminder of the co-operation between town and army and attracts audiences of up to 50,000 people who come from all over the world to see it, with both civilian and army charities benefitting.

Apart from the constant reminder of war due to the presence of the army and the brief alarm during the Napoleonic period, the population of Colchester was able to live peacefully enough from the end of the Siege until the outbreak of the First World War. Then, in 1914, the whole of Colchester was turned into an armed camp. Reservists thronged the Camp pitched in Abbey Field and armed guards were placed on duty outside the Post Office and at the Water Tower and East Mill. Troops passing through were quartered at the Corn Exchange and billeted throughout the town. The town felt the effects in other ways too — League Football was suspended and even the Oyster Feast was abandoned for the duration. Parts of both the Castle Park and the Recreation Ground were turned into allotments in the 'Dig for Victory' campaign and the ubiquitous flour pudding made its first appearance.

In January 1915, instructions for evacuation were sent to every citizen of Colchester, though they were prefaced by some reassuring words: "It is not more likely now than it has been at any previous time during the war that a landing will be effected, but in the improbable event of this happening, the Military Authorities may find it necessary . . . to give instructions to leave the Town".

A regimental parade in the old Goojerat Barracks before they were knocked down and rebuilt in the 1920s.

The signal to leave was to be three rockets sent up from the Town Hall three times at intervals of five minutes. Enough food to last for forty-eight hours was to be taken. The evacuation routes were through Lexden to Chitt's Hill and then on to Haverhill.

In May 1916, new instructions were issued which were not quite so reassuring, as they now stated: "An attempt at invasion is not at all improbable, and its temporary success is not impossible"! The new route provided for evacuation to Saffron Walden. Motor cars were allowed provided that "such vehicles have not been commandeered by the Military Authorities or the Police."

As the war progressed evacuation routes got longer and longer — the next went through Saffron Walden to Royston. The instructions also got more and more detailed. By 1917, it was stated that, in the event of an emergency, "Bicycle shops and provision shops should be emptied and contents distributed to the people." Also that "No destruction whatever is to take place without a special order from the Military Authorities . . . an order to destroy may comprise all or any of the following items:

a) Live stock. The best way to kill cattle is to shoot them.
b) Grain Stock.
c) Hay stocks and straw stocks.
d) Petrol."

The instructions then added helpfully: "Alcoholic liquors need not be destroyed."

For Colcestrians living through the period the main day to day problem facing them was one of food. By the end of the war, butter, margarine, lard, tea, sugar, bacon and meat were all rationed. Sugar, in particular, became the source of some friction between shopkeeper and consumer. In 1917, the Colchester Food Economy Campaign reported that "traders are not quite fair to the poorer classes" and successfully prosecuted one trader for profiteering at their expense.

The Campaign Committee were, however, worried that proper constraint was not being shown in the consumption of bread. In reply to an enquiry as to if the request to limit consumption of bread was being carried out, the Secretary to the Committee replied "With the Upper Middle Classes yes. The cottager class I fear are at present making little effort to assist. One of our lady canvassers was bluntly told 'there always was enough bread and always would be.' " He went on to suggest that bakers and confectioners should exhibit food substitutes on alternate days to take the place of wheat products. "Really," he declared firmly, "this should be compulsory."

Meanwhile, the Colchester War Kitchen in St. Mary Magdalene Parish Hall, Wimpole Road, was doing a roaring trade. On one day, May 16th, 1917, they bought fifty-six portions of topside (20¾lb) for £1 11s 1½d and sold them for £1 17s 4d as well as five quarts of milk for 2s 1d and six bundles of rhubarb for 1s 0d.

Although suffering from some deprivations themselves, the people of Colchester did not forget those even less fortunate and through the Essex Regiment Prisoners of War Fund they managed to send food parcels through to Germany. One typically grateful leter of thanks was received from Sergeant A. H. Blowers of the 2nd Battalion Essex Regiment, imprisoned in Kriegsfangenenlager, Sprottau. Dated October 6th, 1918, and written to the Mayor of Colchester, it reported that Parcel 13 containing "Ox cheek and veg., rhubarb pudding, fresh herrings, milk, dripping, corn flour, sugar, bacon, chocolate, tea, soap, prunes, 2 soups and a cocoa tablet" had arrived safely.

As the war progressed more and more wounded soldiers returned home. In the end, the Essex County Hospital could not cope with the numbers, so a school building was equipped as a hospital for women and children to free the County Hospital wards for the soldiers. Two large huts were also erected in the grounds doubling the accommodation available. Wounded troops were entertained at the Borough Social Club in the Public Hall, supplied free of charge by the Essex and Suffolk Fire Insurance Society. The soldiers could pass the time reading, writing, playing billiards, chess or draughts. Light refreshments, cigarettes, stamps and postal orders were on sale and thirteen baths installed. The Hall was also used as a local food office, war pensioners enquiry office, the Mayoress's Needlework Centre and the Soldiers and Sailors Families Association Office.

What finally brought the war home to the people of Colchester in the most emphatic way possible was the dropping of some of the first bombs ever to be dropped anywhere in England. It was on the beautiful moonlit Sunday night of February 21st, 1915, that a Taube found its way to the Essex Coast, flew up over Brightlingsea and, at 8.40p.m., dropped four bombs in the vicinity of Butt Road, Colchester. Only one caused any damage when it fell into the back garden of Quatermaster-Sergeant Rabjohn at 41 Butt Road. Rabjohn of the 20th Hussars,

Red Cross volunteers practising at Old Heath School during the First World War.

later gave his account of what happened:

> "We had a marvellous escape, my wife, baby, and myself. My wife was standing at the table preparing supper. Unexpectedly and before we could realise what was happening there was a horrible thud which seemed to shake the house. It made in fact a devil of a noise.
>
> "At the same moment there was an immense cloud of brick and dust which covered and blinded me. I at once tumbled to the state of affairs. I rushed to the corner and turned the gas off. My wife meanwhile had turned dizzy. I seized her and rapidly brought her round. She said 'Go up for baby,' and going up to the bedroom we were overjoyed to find the child still sleeping as if nothing at all had occurred. Only then did we realise fully that our home was wrecked."

Although there was a substantial amount of damage, the only reported casualty was a thrush "rudely slaughtered," as the *Essex County Standard* somewhat sensationally reported, "by a shower of German shrapnel."

The air-raid on Colchester on February 21st, 1915, showing the extent of the damage to Sergeant Rabjohn's garden.

At the time there were no black-out precautions and, even after the bombs fell, the lights stayed on all over Colchester except in the nearby barracks, which was assumed at the time to have been the real target of the attack. Assumed that is by all except a correspondent to the *Standard* who reported the following curious story:

> "Nearly two years ago a resident was walking past the house in Butt Road ... when a hawker — evidently a German — retreated from the doorway in high dudgeon at his solicitations having been pre-emptorily refused. He gave vent to his indignation by denouncing, in a marked German accent, not only the occupant of the house but also her nationality. He concluded his maledictions with words to the effect: 'All right. You wait. We are making guns and ammunition for you English night and day.' It is certainly an extraordinary coincidence that the only sample of German explosive ammunition that has been dropped in the neighbourhood of Colchester should have fallen within a few yards of the very house which received the angry denunciation of the German hawker two years ago."

All the way from Germany to exact revenge with such pinpoint accuracy!

The story did have a happy ending when a new perambulator was presented to the Rabjohns by Lady Colebrooke who bought the replacement pram at Harrod's. "I want it to be a really good one," she said.

Although this incident happened fairly early on in the war and dire warnings were issued by the Town Clerk from time to time —"DANGER FROM AIR RAIDS ... TAKE SHELTER IN THE NEAREST BUILDING," screamed one poster dated June 2nd, 1917 — there were, in fact, very few air-raids. Perhaps the worst one came in 1917 when eleven Zeppelins flew over the town and dropped bombs. Trams were held up for five hours. One of the Zeppelins was brought down at Old Heath. Previous to that, on September 23rd, 1916, a Zeppelin came down at Little Wigborough and the whole crew were captured by a solitary Special Constable, Edgar Nicholls. They were taken first to Mersea Island and then to Colchester to await internment.

One of the effects of the air-raids was the introduction of the black-out. This led to many difficulties in getting around but nowhere was there a more unforseen hazard than on the railways. Notices put up in railway carriages at the time read:

> "At night time, when the blinds are drawn, Passengers are requested before alighting to make sure THAT THE TRAIN IS AT REST AT THE PLATFORM."

The final bout of rationing came on November 3rd, 1918, when jam, marmalade, syrup, treacle and honey were all placed on the restricted list. Just eight days later the war ended.

As soon as the armistice was announced crowds quickly thronged the main roads waving Union Jacks. The mayor ordered all the lights turned on and, it is said, that the younger children were greatly impressed by their first sight of street lighting.

The peace celebrations took place on July 6th 1919, when a triumphal march to the Town Hall took place with a Grand *Fête* on Abbey Field in the afternoon and a concert in Castle Park as well as sports on the Land Lane Ground. The evening was lit up by fireworks and military flares. At night the townspeople returned to their homes full of optimism that the "war to end all wars" was finally over and that an everlasting peace stretching on into infinity now lay before them.

Unfortunately it was not to be. Just twenty years later, on September 3rd, 1939, Britain was again at war, with Colchester back in the front line. The first air-raid siren sounded at 3.05a.m. on September 4th, only hours after war had been declared. Even at that early hour many people came out of their homes to see if they could see anything. Those that did heard two planes flying high overhead. Two days later the sirens went again. By the end of 1939, the siren had sounded five times and the scene was already set for six grim years. The town's character changed completely as the lights went out and peacetime activities came to a standstill. Sandbags were piled up outside public buildings, signs were taken down and windows were plastered with sticky paper. Gas detector paint was on every pillar box and everyone had to carry their gas mask. Shop fronts filled up with notices: 'No Matches", "No Sugar", No this; no that. Household notices were issued — "W" for water — and stirrup pumps were issued for dealing with incendiary bombs. All bus journeys after 9p.m. were cancelled and all Sunday services before 1p.m. also stopped.

There was khaki everywhere as more and more men were called up for active service. Rationing came back and both adults and children left the town —

The crew of Zeppelin L. 33 being taken to Colchester by the lone special Edgar Nicholls who, according to a local eye-witness, ''took up the whole of 'em''.

Women workers aiding the war effort at Paxman's by making shell cases during the First World War.

evacuated mostly to the Midlands. Air-raids increased in intensity throughout 1940 as the Battle of Britain was fought out over the skies of East Anglia. The Colcestrians that remained were able to look up and witness some amazing scenes, such as the battles on August 31st and September 3rd, 1940, when Hurricanes and Spitfires took on the might of the German *Luftwaffe* and the sky was streaked with bullets and screaming aircraft ducking and weaving to gain the best advantage.

On the ground entertainments had been cut to the minimum, Colchester United played no football from Christmas 1940 until 1945. The Colchester Repertory Company finished in the Spring of 1940 and went off to entertain the troops. There was unease, rumour and suspicion. Stories spread that there were spies around and a sombre and uneasy mood settled over Colchester.

But there were jobs to be done and soon the spirit of comradeship reasserted itself and people organised themselves into volunteer groups to guard their houses from fire attacks. Many who joined had never even seen a large fire let alone fought one. The W.V.S. expanded its activities. It organised home visits to collect salvage in response to Lord Beaverbrook's exhortation to the "Women of Britain" to turn their "pots and pans into Spitfires and Hurricanes." The Womens' Institute held special jam-making and bottling sessions. School grounds were used for allotments in the "Dig for Victory" Campaign and £50,000 was raised to buy a destroyer.

Gradually people grew accustomed to the black-outs and the air-raids. The Colchester Repertory Company returned and in December 1940, Colchester was excluded from the Coastal Defence Area, which meant a further relaxation of restrictions. Humour reappeared on the shop front signs — instead of "NO" there was "We keep open during alerts, except in the event of a direct hit, when we close at once."

And, although the deprivation continued — by the end of the year onions, lemons, eggs, slab chocolate, tinned milk and bananas were no longer available — the new spirit enabled Colcestrians to face whatever was thrown at them with a new courage and a feeling of comradeship.

Every house was issued with a card with green numbers on it, 1-6. One of these numbers had to be cut out and placed in the window to show how many members of the household were still living there. This was to help rescue workers in the event of a bomb scoring a direct hit. One person who remembers having to put up the number 1 was Mrs Lawrence, who was a cook at a nearby school, which by now had been turned into a canteen. She remembers a joint exercise taking place to see how prepared the civilian population were in the event of an emergency. Her job was to make the stew and apple pies. She recalls that the only casualty was herself when she burnt her arm in the stew!

When the Batte of Britain came to an end the nature of the war in the air also changed. From watching fighters fighting it out, Colcestrians now had to look out for bombers bombing their town and their houses. Some tragic raids took place, such as the one on October 3rd, 1940, when three girls were killed at a laundry and, worst of all, the one in 1942, when thirty-eight people were killed at Severalls Hospital. The worst hit area was around St. Botolph's, where, on February 23rd, 1944, a rain of phosphorus bombs destroyed over a dozen

Civil Defence Volunteers with stirrup pumps at the ready! Taken in the grounds of Old Heath School during the Second World War. Air-raid shelter in background.

houses, two factories and a furniture store. In all more than a hundred fires were started that night. Some raids seemed to be particularly meaningless and cruel such as the time when German planes machine-gunned children in the playground at Harwich Road School.

In all fifty-four people were killed in air-raids on Colchester, over a thousand injured and fifty houses entirely destroyed. Between that first air-raid on September 4th, 1939, and the last one at the end of March, 1945, there were 1093 air-raids and 685 warnings of crashing aircraft. The longest continuous warning was one of 9 hours 50 minutes on the night of September 23rd/24th, 1940. And from September 13th, 1940 until October 23rd, 1940, there was an air-raid warning on every night except two.

Black-out restrictions were eventually lifted on April 23rd, 1945, and news of the end of the war itself reached Colchester at 3.15p.m. on May 7th, 1945, at the offices of the *Essex County Standard.* Unlike 1918 there was no immediate taking to the streets when the news came through. There was a general feeling of thanksgiving, but most remembered that a numer of Colcestrians were still fighting out in the Far East or were in Japanese prisoner-of-war camps. Nevertheless flags went up and bunting appeared everywhere. The *Essex County Standard* at the time stated: ''The hotels wre crowded — in many cases it was total surrender to our American Allies.'' (Whatever that's supposed to mean!)

The following day, May 8th, was designated VE Day, when crowds at last swarmed on to the streets to hear the Prime Minister's speech being broadcast and relayed from the Town Hall. In the afternoon celebrations took place in Abbey Fields and thousands of people took part in impromptu sports and sideshows.

On VE night the crowds returned to the High Street to dance, sing and cheer while the town was swept with searchlights. In the following days most streets held street parties to celebrate Colchester's freedom and deliverance from the terrible nightmare of the previous six years.

J. SAINSBURY
J. SAINSBURY.
BLACKFRIARS
W.J. HARRIS & Co
BUTTER
J. SAINSBURY.
PROVISIONS
J. SAINSBURY.
WRINGER & MANGLE
A SEWING MACHINE
KODAK

Shops

If you had gone shopping in Colchester in 1880 you would have had a wide variety of shops to choose from. They were mostly small shops where the shopkeeper lived over the premises and the servants lived in — the multinationals had not yet arrived. Some interesting names and shops of that period included Ebeneezer Orrin, Boot & Shoe Maker of St. John's Street; Joseph Shepherd, Tinman of Osborne Street; Isaac Tatam, Firewood Dealer of Bromley Road; Elizabeth Wheeler, Wardrobe Dealer of Military Road, Henry Ambrose, taxidermist of North Street; John Bird, Grindery Dealer of Magdalen Street; and the up-to-date Frederick Braess, Photographer of Sir Isaac's Walk. What is perhaps even more interesting, looking back over 100 years, is that the following also existed in the Colchester of 1880: Ben Cant, Rose Grower of St. John's Street; George Griffen, Cabinet Maker, Upholsterer, Paperhanger and Church Furnisher of High Street; Lay & Wheeler, Wine & Spirit, Ale & Porter Merchants of High Street; Charles Tweed, Baker of North Street; George & Henry Farmer, Cutlers of High Street; Frederick Mann, Musical Instrument Maker of St. John's Street and Kent & Blaxill, Oil, Colour & Window Glass Merchants & Brush Dealers of High Street.

During the 1880s a number of now well-known shops were to appear in Colchester. Shops such as:

CULLINGFORD's which was started as a newsagent and stationers by Richard Wincup Cullingford at 54 North Hill in the early months of 1885. He moved to 153 High Street in 1886 and was joined in 1888 by a compositor called Frank Bloom when the printing side of the business got underway. This expanded rapidly and by 1900, Cullingford's was producing the first of its annual *Cullingford's Street Directory*. These lasted for fifteen years. In 1904, a lease was taken out on the shop at 156 High Street, the site where Cullingford's have remained to this day. By 1913, Cullingford's were paying their craftsmen £1 15s per week. Working Hours were from 8.00a.m. — 6.30p.m., with a 1½ hour lunch break, Monday to Friday and 8.00a.m. — 1.00p.m. on Saturday. Two weeks unpaid holiday per year was allowed. In their set of rules for employees the following appeared: ''Anyone entering or leaving work surreptitiously will be fined a shilling for the offence and for the second will be discharged''!

◀ Sainsburys as it looked in 1928. In 1932 it extended into the adjacent shop.

The shop and printing works continued to expand throughout the 20th Century and in 1961 they won the *Printing World* National Typesetting Award. In 1967, the shop expanded when the old St. George's Hall passage was taken into the shop and it is from this time that the present shop front dates.

HATFIELD's: Begun by John Hatfield, a ''dealer in curios'' in 1886 at 31 St. John's Street. Although his record system was somewhat primitive — he noted his customers orders on his shirt cuffs — the business expanded. In December 1916, he paid £500 for the adjoining properties of 32-34 St. John's Street, which also included nos. 4-6 Sir Isaac's Walk.

In 1935, Arthur Hatfield (John's son) sold the St. John's Street shop and continued to trade from the Hatfield's former warehouse at 5 Stanwell Street (now part of Osborne Street), where they were to continue until 1981. For many years Hatfield's continued as a *curios* and second-hand furniture dealer. David London, now a director of Hatfield's, recalls that he had the problem of clearing the stockroom in the early 1960s and found ''buckets full of false teeth, spectacles, keys, piles and piles of broken china, clothing and books'' as well as two empty coffins.

In 1957, with a hardware department already started, Hatfield's acquired a building at 1 George Street and used this as a furniture showroom. When Parker Knoll agreed to supply them with new furniture, Hatfield's entered a new era. Carpets were added in 1962 and although second-hand furniture was still being sold, Hatfield's was now becoming Colchester's leading supplier of new furniture.

On November 22nd, 1962, the shop expanded yet again into new premises at the end of St. Botolph's Street. Total takings for the opening day at the new shop amounted to £59 19s 6d.

Hatfield's continued to expand and began to look around for larger premises. Eventually they took the momentous decision to move out of the town centre and on August 27th, 1976, the present shop at Peartree Road was opened by the Mayor of Colchester, Cllr. Joyce Brooks.

Shops already existing in 1880 included:

KENT, BLAXILL: John Kent opened the forerunner of Kent, Blaxill as far back as 1838 at 104 High Street. Seven customers came into his shop on that first day and his takings at the end of his first week came to £10 6s. Those same premises stayed in the hands of Kent and then Kent, Blaxill for 128 years.

In 1844 John Kent added glass to his oil and colour business and, as the boom of the 1880s came, Kent & Blaxill (as the shop had become in 1878) were well placed to take advantage. By 1905 the firm had grown so large that it was agreed to turn it into a Private Limited Liability Company. Throughout the early years of the century and the 20s and 30s the shop became one of the most well-known in Colchester and had a unique atmosphere. The smell of the oils and varnishes gave the shop a characteristic all its own.

On the afternoon of May 24th, 1952, a disastrous fire destroyed the Kent, Blaxill premises, now expanded to 101-104 High Street, and caused almost £70,000 worth of damage. Fortunately they had other premises — at 3 High

B. & L. Noy, the Brass Band shop in North Hill. B. & L. Noy actually started life as a confectioners during the First World War but, for some reason, turned their attention to musical instruments in the 1920s.

Street, 60 High Street and 121 High Street — and so were able to continue trading almost normally. It was not until March 1955, almost three years later, that 101-104 High Street was again open for business.

With the rapid expansion of business, Kent, Blaxill were on the desperate look-out for new premises. With space at a premium inside Colchester they decided to move out of the town centre and on September 30th, 1963, a thousand people witnessed the official opening of the Layer Road warehouse. The premises at 101-104 High Street were sold on January 2nd, 1967.

Today, as well as paint and glass, Kent, Blaxill stock wallpaper, kitchen furniture, sanitaryware, baths, boilers, radiators, bricks, blocks and anything else the building trade might want.

LAY & WHEELER: Founded as a wine merchant in July 1854 by John Lay at 97 High Street, his total stock amounted to £300 worth of wine and £100 worth of spirits. He moved to 10 High Street in 1862, where the back of the site still forms the present Lay & Wheeler premises in Culver Street. In 1873, George Wheeler became a partner and the shop became known as Lay & Wheeler. The business soon boomed and it is reputed that on Christmas Eve 1914, the queue of soldiers trying to get in stretched from the front door all the way round into Head Street.

In 1937 the stables and cart shed at the rear of the shop in Culver Street were converted into the present-day shop and offices.

COLCHESTER CO-OP: The first shop was opened on August 9th, 1861, in Culver Street and sold butter for one shilling per pound and sugar for four or five pence per pound. In 1878, the Co-op added boots and drapery to its stock and built a bakery at New Town. With the building expansion of the 1880s, the Co-op opened a new grocery in North Station Road at a cost of £400. Further shops were opened in and around Colchester and by 1903 the membership stood at 6,300, and by 1911, over two hundred people worked in Co-op shops.

In 1954, Saint Nicholas Church in the High Street was sold at public auction for £88,000 and subsequently demolished. In 1956 the new Co-op Department Store began to take shape on the site and finally opened there in 1957. Further expansion followed and a five acre site was acquired at Stanway in 1965.

Robert Hall's shop on the corner of North Hill and High Street, a site it occupied for almost the whole of the nineteenth century.

These shops are some of Colchester's own curent local success stories. A 19th century success was the shop on the corner of High Street and North Hill, ROBERT J. HALLS, which first appeared in the 1823/4 *Pigot Directory* as a Fruiterer & Oyster Packer. Over the next eighty years, the shop was variously described as a Fishmonger, Dealer in Game, Poulterer and, at one time in 1882, as an assessor of taxes for St. Peter's Parish. These descriptions appeared at different times and in different combinations. The shop was eventually taken over by W. W. Scott, Fishmonger, Poulterer, Game Dealer and Ice Merchant in about 1900.

Perhaps Robert J. Hall himself lasted the eighty years just as in our time Mr F. V. Cheek, Greengrocer and Miscellaneous Salesman, did at the bottom of Scheregate. His shop survived from 1907 until November 30th, 1988, when he eventually decided to retire. He was six when he first moved in with his parents, and, at the age of eighty-seven, when he finally called it a day, he could still be seen every day cycling to work.

From the 1880s right up until the 1950s, shops had to vie for custom, not only with the street markets but also with itinerent street sellers. One well-remembered street seller was Clarence who sold Yarmouth bloaters for a penny each or seven for sixpence. One way of attracting custom was to advertise in the local paper as E. Hammerton of 28 High Street did in 1880: ''Aromatic Ginger Ale. A winter beverage, warming and refurbishing.'' or, more reassuringly, Messrs Buck & Dixon of 27 Head Street: ''Messrs Buck & Dixon beg to inform friends and patients that they continue to supply Artificial teeth ... operations performed by means of pure Nitro Oxide Gas ...''

As well as advertising, the shopkeepers attracted and kept custom by keeping their shops clean and tidy and by adhering to the old saying: ''The customer is always right.'' There was no rush round the supermarket with a trolley, grabbing pre-packaged goods as you went. Who of that generation, cannot remember the butter being patted out in front of you so you could see exactly what and how much you were getting, or the ham sliced off the bone or the cheese cut with the wire cheese cutter? Paying for goods too was not a matter of an electronic device reading a computerised bar code (whatever that is!) You knew exactly what you were paying for and how much. At Sainsbury's the shop assistant would give the customer a ticket. The customer would then go across to the pay office, pay and then go back to collect the goods. The Co-op had the overhead containers that powered by compressed air sent your money flying across the shop to the cashier, as did Lucking's at the bottom of St. Botolph's Street. People waited and were happy to wait. There was a tomorrow after all.

By the turn of the century, some of the big chain stores were being attracted to the expanding town of Colchester. One of the first was BOOTS who opened up on the corner of Long and Short Wyre Streets around the turn of the century.

SAINSBURYS arrived in 1905 when a counter-service shop opened at 41 High Street. It sold ham, cooked meats, pies and sausages from the long narrow counter on one side of the shop and cheese, butter and eggs from the other side. It expanded in 1932 to No. 40 next door. Even with two shops it became apparent that larger premises were needed if a proper range of products was to be offered, and so a new supermarket was opened in 1969 at 8/13 Kingsway. At the time it was Sainsbury's second largest store in the country.

In 1979, a new branch was opened at Lexden, and this itself was replaced in 1987, when, on February 24th of that year, a new supermarket at Tollgate was opened.

MARKS & SPENCER arrived at 3 St. Botolph's Street in 1911 with their "Penny Bazaar". On April 17th, 1931, they moved to their current site at 38/39 High Street (next door to the old Sainsbury's). They expanded several times, including taking over the Sainsbury site when that store moved. In 1965 they opened up a rear entrance on to Culver Street, so that by 1975 they were in a prime position to take advantage of the new Lion Walk Shopping Precinct which they did by expanding into one of the units, becoming one of the first two shops to open in the precinct.

Sainsbury's staff ready to serve in 1936.

◀ Sainsbury's newly opened shop in the High Street, 1910.

HARRIS&Co
The JOSCELIN CAFE
SALVAGE STOCK
37

Marks & Spencer's first shop — the Penny Bazarre — in St. Botolph's Street shortly after its opening in 1911. On the right is Pipers who were drapers and haberdashers. The shop assistants lived with the owners above the shop as part of the family.

◀ You'd need to have a good memory to remember 38/39 High Street looking like this! But this is what it looked like in 1930 just before the arrival of Marks & Spencer.

Marks & Spencer's new shop in the High Street, which opened on April 17th, 1931.

F. W. WOOLWORTH, with a bit of unfortunate timing, brought his ''3d and 6d Stores'' to Colchester at the outbreak of World War 1. Woolworth's remained at 49 High Street throughout their existence in Colchester, pausing only to expand either side into Nos. 48 and 50. In 1965 the store was completely rebuilt and remodelled. However, it only lasted another 20 years, as a Head Office rationalisation scheme closed it down in the 1980s. Rumour has it that Woolworth's are now looking to return to Colchester . . .

With the arrival of Lion Walk Precinct many fears were expressed over the future of the High Street. Most of the big shops either moved into it from the High Street, or new ones opened there. Marks & Spencer, Boots, W. H. Smith, British Home Stores, Dixon, Rumbelow are just a few who took advantage of the precinct. The fear was that far from providing extra shopping, all that would happen was that shoppers would gravitate there instead of using the High Street. The President of the Colchester Chamber of Trade and Commerce, Mr. John O'Halloran, articulated this fear when he said that although Lion Walk had been successful, it ''has had the effect of concentrating more customers to the east of the town than is fair. The High Street has suffered as a result and was in danger of becoming a back-water''. In an attempt to find out the true position a survey was carried out in 1978 of customers entering Marks & Spencer. It was found that exactly the same numbers entered from both the High Street end and the Lion Walk entrance. (Though how many just used it to walk straight through without doing any shopping at all was not revealed).

The fears for the High Street were accelerated by the rapid growth of out of town shopping facilities. Perhaps the major event that typified those fears was the curious story of Tesco. Following the creation of Southway and the restoration of St. John's Street to pedestrians, Tesco opened a brand new large supermarket there in 1981. It helped turn the street from a depressed area into a booming part of the town. To facilitate this, the company closed its twenty year old shop in Head Street. Almost simultaneously, they opened a new £2million superstore at High Woods, closing another shop in Wyncolls Road. High Woods proved to be an amazing success story and within six years Tescos had closed its St. John's Street store to concentrate its efforts at High Woods, thus abandoning the town centre.

With Sainsburys, Tescos and even local shops such as Kent, Blaxill and Hatfields moving out the pattern had been set. The return of the market to the High Street did help, but the Street has lost much of its former variety. Many of the shops are now banks or building societies or fast food outlets. The new Culver Street Shopping Precinct has attracted C & As and Debenhams and yet another large out-of-town establishment — Tollgate at Stanway — has attracted Bejam, Comet, Allied Carpets and Wallace King. Is there anything left for the proposed new Head Street Precinct to attract?

The nature of shopping has changed dramatically over the last twenty years. The chain stores have arrived with a vengeance, while a number of the old established Colchester shops have risen to the challenge admirably. The motor car and the pace of modern life have largely been responsible for this change. It will be very interesting to see what changes the next twenty years will bring.

21-22 GRAFTON ST. DUBLIN
BURTON
BILL
HA
F.W. WOOLWORTH & Co. LTD. 3D. AND 6D. STORES
F.W. WOOLWORTH & Co. LTD 3D & 6D STORES
NOTHING IN THESE STORES OVER 6D
F.W. WOOLWORTH & Co. LTD 3D & 6D STORES

Woolworths after complete remodelling had taken place in 1965.

◀ F. W. Woolworth & Co. Ltd. 3d & 6d Stores in the early 1920s.

An impressive bit of Paxman's engineering shown off by its proud workers around 1910.

Industry

Following the collapse of Colchester's cloth industry in the eighteenth century agriculture took over as the staple element of the town's economy. Rural industries such as milling and brewing grew up alongside, and, in particular, Wilson Marriage, son of the founder Edward Marriage, at East Mill built up a very modern business, installing steam engines as early as the 1870s and later on roller-mills. The business continued to expand until it was finally taken over by the Hovis-Rank-MacDougall combine. East Mill itself is now thriving as a hotel.

In brewing, the local industry came to be dominated by three firms, Daniell's of Maidenburgh Street; East Hill Brewery and the Colchester Brewing Company, also of East Hill. By 1900 the three companies between them owned approximately 500 licensed houses mostly in North Essex. Of these, the largest, the Colchester Brewing Company (formerly known as the Eagle Brewery) supplied 250. This company lasted until well into the 1920s when it was taken over by Ind Coope.

However, it was the engineering industry that was to form the backbone of Colchester's economic boom of the 1880s. A number of small foundries had started in the mid-1800s to provide tools and machinery for the farmers and millers. As agriculture began to slump this dependence on such customers became very dangerous and many saw the need to escape. Joseph Bloomfield at St. Botolph's, for example, began making velocipedes and sewing machines in 1861. This firm later became the Britannia Engineering Company, at one time even turning out motor cars. Ironically, the site of its former factory is now a car park.

Only one firm, Cathchpool, Stannard and Stannard of the High Street, continued to turn out threshing machines and other farm equipment to the exclusion of all else.

From 1865 onwards, however, one firm began to dominate the engineering scene in Colchester. This was the year in which James Noah Paxman joined with Henry and Charles Davey to found "Davey, Paxman and Davey, Engineers". Their first factory was called the "Standard Ironworks" and was situated in Culver Street. Shortly after seting up their establishment, Davey, Paxman and Davey gave over part of their works to Arthur G. Mumford. When the Davey brothers retired in 1876, James Paxman moved his Standard Ironworks to Hythe Quay. Arthur Mumford stayed at Culver Street until 1933 and became one of Britain's leading manufacturers of marine pumps and engines and supplied the British, Russian and Italian navies.

Paxman's early products still included some agricultural machinery and mill gearing but they gradually began to move into boilers and steam engines and then into a most profitable area with mining equipment. For many years, Paxman's supplied the Kinberley Diamond Mines with winding and hauling machinery.

By the turn of the century, Paxman's was well into the manufacture of steam engines and in 1923 they built a railway goods locomotive for the Ravenglass and Eskdale Railway.

As well as becoming Colchester's leading manufacturer and exporter, Paxman's was also known as a model employer. They provided good working conditions and sports and social facilities. Their sports ground near East Mill was one of the best in Colchester and their sports day one of Colchester's main annual events. In 1930 a skilled craftsman earned between £2. 10s and £2 12s per week.

When the war came in 1939, Paxman's worked flat out to provide the necessary war materials, in particular a marine propulsion unit. One hair-raising story of those war years occurred when a Paxman engineer called Eric Rowe was flown out to neutral Sweden in the bomb rack of a Mosquito. His job was to repair engines and to maintain the vital link with Swedish industry which was supplying ball-bearings for the British aircraft industry. Unfortunately Mr. Rowe lost his tools when the ship that was taking them over was sunk. He therefore went to look for some more and was told by a Swedish friend that there was a retailer in a nearby town. Together they called at the address given but they soon realised that there had been some mistake as they were shown into a magnificent apartment. Turning on his friend, Mr. Rowe was interrupted in perfect English by the occupant of the apartment who turned out to be the German counsul!

Another important task undertaken by Paxman's during the war was the repairing and reconditioning of engines which had been damaged through enemy action.

Following the war, the company continued to grow and moved into the full-scale production of diesel engines. In 1966 Paxman became part of the English Electric Diesel group and then in 1968 part of the giant G.E.C. combine. Today it manufactures engines for Royal Navy ships, North Sea oil rigs, the United States Coastguards, British Rail (including the 125 train), the Australian Railway and for industry in general throughout the world. It is currently the largest employer in the area.

Another highly successful company has been the Colchester Lathe Co., a relative late-comer, not being established until 1907 by John Ephraim Cohen. The original works were approximately 100 feet square with four offices and two toilets. These works were situated on what today is still part of the present factory at the Hythe.

The company started up in direct opposition to the Britannia Company. In its early years it employed about fifty people and produced four or five lathes per week. Wages in 1914 were twenty-four shillings per week for a skilled tradesman and eighteen shillings per week for a labourer.

In 1921 the company bought its first demonstration van which toured the country seeking out new orders. This proved to be highly successful.

In the 1920s heating was provided by means of ''Tortoise Stoves''. Most employees used these to bake chestnuts or potatoes (strictly against regulations).

After the war building expansion took place with great urgency, and in 1954 the company became part of the 600 Group. In 1962 a new factory was built at Elmstead Road, though the main operations continued and still continue at the Hythe Works, where the Headstock factory was opened in April 1968.

One other long-standing and successful engineering works in Colchester is that of Woods of Colchester plc, like Paxman's, now part of the G.E.C. Group. They started at the Hythe and are now a leading manufacturer of motors and fans.

For a while, towards the end of the 19th century another industry looked as though it might oust engineering as Colchester's dominant industry. And, indeed, in 1887, John Kavanagh was able to say at a dinner organised by Colchester's railway staff that he presumed he had been invited as he was the largest employer in the town's chief industry, for ''the boot trade was the staple trade of Colchester''.

The first of the large footwear manufacturers was S. G. Knopp who started in 1860 and, after several moves due to the rapid expansion of trade, finally came to rest at the corner of Portland Road and Mersea Road (near the present roundabout) in 1868. There he built his ''Time Will Tell'' factory — three stories high with a tall chimney announcing to the world that this was ''Knopp & Son, Wholesale Boot Manufaturers''. In 1880 they were advertising their ''celebrated Standard Screw Boots'' made by screwing not rivetting, and later their welted boots which ''do not creak when walking''.

The second large manufacturer was John Kavanagh. Although entering the field later than Knopp, he had, by 1887, overtaken him as the industry's largest employer. He specialised in army ware and, by the late 1880s, was coping with the reconditioning of 2,700 pairs of army boots per week. In 1890 he opened Colchester's most modern factory to date — a ''lofty and spacious structure''. In that factory 300 employees made 170,000 pairs of boots annually plus repairing 100,000 pairs of army boots. Internal telephones were installed in the building and lifts connected the various floors.

The last major boot and shoe factory was A. C. George's on the corner of Kendall Road and Charles Street. He also had two retail outlets in the High Street.

By 1897 there were just under 1000 employees altogether in Colchester's footwear industry. Yet, incredibly, and for no apparent reason, it had completely collapsed by 1909 — Kavanagh's closed in 1898, George in 1908 and Knopp in 1909.

Other local industry has included Hyam's clothing factory, Pertwee Holdings Ltd. and Owen Parry's oil mills, which started life as Owen Parry ''oil cake manufacturer'' of the Hythe in about 1890. But it was undoubtedly engineering that was to provide the solid basis for Colchester's economic revival of the 1880s and for its sustained position ever since.

The 100,000th Colchester Lathe being turned out in 1970. Fifth from the left is Jack Mitchell, the Works Director and next to him Leslie Webster, the Managing Director.

An early newspaper advert for Knopp & Son.

◀ By the 1960s Colchester Lathe's publicity and advertising van had turned into a bus. Here it is being hoisted aboard ship for an overseas tour in 1961.

The Mayor hauls up the first catch of the season from the Colchester Oyster Fishery's boat, *Peewit,* in the late 1960s. All aboard then retired for the traditional gin and gingerbread celebrations!

Sid Westwood packing oysters ready for the London Market. Sid has worked for the Colchester Oyster Fishery since 1965. Before then he ''messed about on the water'' for a living. Behind Sid are the purifying tanks.

Oysters and Roses

Two other Colchester industries which deserve a special mention of their own are oysters and roses.

The oyster industry is without a doubt Colchester's oldest, dating as it does at least back to Roman times and probably even further. When the Borough of Colchester was granted its Royal Charter in 1189 it was also granted the rights to the ''fishery of the Colne and its creeks''. Over the centuries several individuals challenged this exclusive right but subsequent Charters continued to confirm the Borough's rights.

In 1758, however, an Act of Parliament placed the fishery under the control of the Justices of the Peace and they leased the river to the dredgermen. Unfortunately the fishery was not well managed and stocks of oysters dwindled. In 1807 the Colne Fishery Company was formed and they made an all-out effort to restock the Colne. At first the efforts were successful but owing to mismanagement and distrust between the company and the Corporation things began to go awry and in 1870 another Act of Parliament gave control of the fishery back to the Corporation but left the company in charge of the management and working of the fishery.

This new arrangement worked satisfactorily until 1962-3 when the bitter winter almost finished off the stocks of oysters completely and the Colne Fishery Company folded. Just one man, Jack Francis, the foreman, kept his faith in the industry and he remained as caretaker bailiff until a new lease was let in 1965 to Colchester Oyster Fishery Limited.

By careful husbandry the few remainig oysters were nurtured until by the late 1960s one hundred and thirty tons of oysters were being harvested annually. The method of cultivation has changed litle over the centuries. Immature oysters are put down in the spring, regularly dredged and culled to fatten them up for the autumn.

Over the last twenty years production of oysters has again dropped. There have been several reasons for this — overfishing, disease from America and several severe winters. Nevertheless, the Colchester oyster is still much sought after and all the top London seafood restaurants could not do without it. The export market is also booming and the Colchester Oyster Fishery Limited's future looks assured for many years to come — perhaps another 2,000?

The town itself celebrates the humble oyster once a year with its world renowned Colchester Oyster Feast. Just when this started is not known, but the earliest mention appears to be in the Chamberlain's accounts for 1667. On the day of the oyster feast, held annually on the eve of St. Denis's Day, the ''bells were rung;

drummers, fifers and musicians were employed; and liquors of various kinds were consumed'' and paid for out of public monies! Until 1845 the oyster feast was for the Mayor, Alderman and Councillors only. In that year the Mayor, Alderman Henry Wolton, invited 200 guests to the feast in the newly-completed Town Hall and set the pattern that has been followed ever since.

At one time, particularly between the wars, the feast reached the proportion of a major national event with royalty, leading politicians, film stars and top sportsmen all making an appearance while crowds filled the street outside hoping to catch a glimpse of their favourites.

Like the Fishery itself, the Feast is not now quite such a major spectacle, but again like the Fishery its future as Colchester's premier annual social event seems assured.

The Colchester Oyster Feast Programme of 1895, designed by W. Gurney Benham.

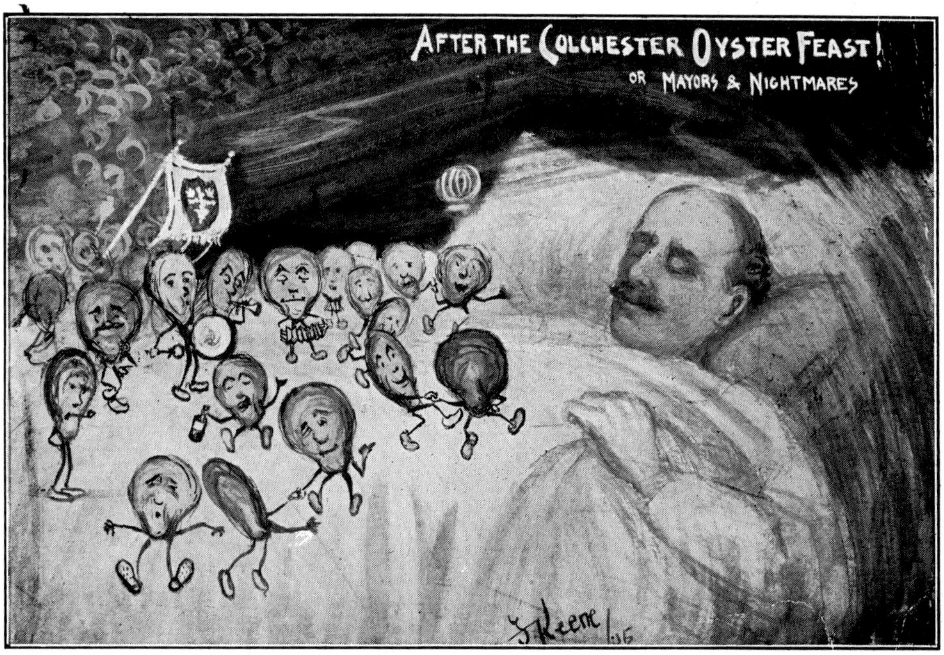

Let's hope this doesn't happen too often.

The Cant family can trace the beginnings of its rose growing industry in Colchester back to 1728 when George Cant, Gardener, was admitted and sworn in as a Free-Burgess of the Borough. And it was circa 1765 when William Cant set up in business on his own as a general nurseryman. It is not known exactly where that first nursery was situated but in the *Colchester Gazette* of September 23rd, 1815, the following advert appeared:

COLCHESTER NURSERY GROUNDS
WILLIAM CANT
BEGS leave to offer . . .
Stock of nursery goods
at his Nursery Grounds, Gutter St., Colchester.

Gutter Street is now St. John's Street.

It was William's grandson Benjamin who discarded the general nursery business in favour of specialising in roses, having been persuaded by the enthusiasm of a Mr. Penrose of Dedham who, in 1853, introduced Benjamin Cant to some new varieties from France. Cant took up the culture of these roses and by 1879 felt able to devote all his time and attention exclusively to the rose.

He was followed by his nephew Frank Cant, who also set up in the business. Benjamin Cant's rose grounds were at Mile End, while Frank's were at Braiswick in the parish of Lexden.

In 1881 the National Rose Society introduced its Champion Challenge Trophy. Between its inauguration and 1899, a space of nineteen years, the Trophy was won by the Cants on no fewer than thirteen occasions, nine times by Benjamin and four by Frank.

By the turn of the century Benjamin Cant was turning out 300,000 plants per year while Frank Cant was turning out in the region of 130,000. Along with the Cants other well-known rose growers such as D. Prior and Osmond Orpen were turning Colchester into the rose capital of England, enabling a contemporary journal to say ''Nowhere else in Englad can the perfect flower of flowers be seen in such amazing quantities as at Colchester''.

The two companies continued to dominate the rose growing scene well into the twentieth century and Benjamin Cant's, the business having by now been taken over by his sons Cecil and Edward, again won the Champion Challenge Trophy in 1905, 1906, 1913, 1914, 1915 and 1918 as well as the Gold Medal of the Royal Horticultural Society in 1920.

In the 1930s Rambler Roses cost between 1s 6d and 2s 6d. The current price is £2.80. Bush roses were 1s 3d in the 30s. Today they are about £2.

For a while, in the 1930s, Benjamin Cant's experimented with perfume made from the roses — ''Ben Cant's Old Rose Perfume'' came in quarter, half and one ounce bottles costing 2s 6d, 3s 6d and 5s 0d respectively. The experiment did not last long, much to the relief of the gardener who was employed to pick the petals! He had had to wear gloves as he kept getting his hands stung by bees.

A part of Frank Cant's rose field at Braiswick in 1905.

In 1939 a new Rose Garden was constructed on the Colchester by-pass and in 1967 the two sides of the family at last merged into one concern when Frank Cant and Benjamin Cant became Cant's of Colchester and moved their head office to Frank Cant's garden centre at Stanway. The new firm continued the old tradition and introduced many new breeds of rose, the most notable being *Alpine Sunset, English Miss* and, the most famous of all, *Just Joey* which in 1986 received the highest award possible for a rose, the James Mason Memorial Trophy, given to the rose that has given the most pleasure to people.

In October 1985, the two sides split again with the Roberts family from the old Frank Cant board continuing to run the Garden Centre, while the Benjamin Cant side returned to their old rose growing business at Mile End.

It is a remarkable fact that, after 260 years, Cant's of Colchester is still in the hands of direct descendents of George Cant. The current chairman is Miss Joan Cant, a granddaughter of Benjamin Cant, while Mr. Clifford Pawsey, who married Miss Diana Cant, another granddaughter, is managing director. Their children are also directors, taking it into yet another generation.

Oysters and Roses have both made a major contribution to the life and economy of Colchester. It is a strange fact that the oyster industry flourishes between September and May, while the rose industry is at its peak between May and September.

In 1905, the Very Rev. S. Reynolds Hole, Dean of Rochester, was a speaker at the Colchester Oyster Feast, which that year was festooned with roses for decoration. He said, ''I suppose there never was an occasion on which there was such a combination of things good to look upon and fit to eat as there are today, a combination of oysters and roses''.

Ben Cant's Roses — a catalogue cover dating from around the turn of the century.

The Hythe in the early years of this century — fairly busy still and not a steamship in sight.

Transport

For centuries, Colchester's main communication with the outside world was by river. And for centuries arguments raged as to who was responsible for keeping the river clear. Over the years the main port of Colchester has moved up and down the river Colne. Possibly as far as Middleborough in one direction and Wivenhoe in the other, By the mid-eighteenth century, the port had more or less settled down in the vicinity of the Hythe and in 1811 an Act of Parliament was procured which made it quite clear who was responsible for the cleansing and upkeep of the Hythe.

Following this, business began to boom and by the 1840s at least five companies were running a weekly or twice-weekly boat service to London, with some companies even running services to Ostend. Steam boats were also gradually beginning to make their appearance. (Though even by 1911 the proportion of sailing boats to steam boats was still something in the order of fifteen to one). Coal merchants were moving their yards to the Hythe, as were corn merchants. The late 1830s and early 1840s were the hey-day for the Hythe and river transport. From then on, apart from brief revivals in the 1860s when the river was deepened as far as East Mill and barges were able to berth alongside the mill, and the 1880s, when again Wilson Marriage became prominent in an attempt to rescue the Hythe, the general position was one of gradual decline. By 1914 voyages in and out fell to only a quarter of what they had been in the early 1890s and by the 1950s business was decidedly slack, with only a certain amount of coal, timber for the timber yards, oil for BP and clay for bricks being brought by river.

Since then there has been a small revival in the river's fortunes when first Fieldgate's and then the Colchester Dock Transit Company started their general cargo businesses. However, as well as the problems caused by the depth of the channel, poor communications from the port inland have militated against too strong a revival. In the late 1960s the railway line into the Hythe was closed and for a while coal was taken to St. Botolph's goods yard for loading and unloading but this proved to be unsuccessful. All transport now goes by road, but links to the Midlands and North are poor.

The size of cargo ships is still growing and it seems likely that within the next ten years, the port will be forced to move once again down river to Wivenhoe, Rowhedge or Fingringhoe if it is to survive.

The other early form of communication with the outside world was the stagecoach. In his *History of Colchester*, written in 1768, Philip Morant stated that Colchester was "an easy day's journey from London, to which a coach goes daily, except Sundays.'' The coach left Colchester at 5a.m. and reached London at 2p.m. By 1838 there were seventeen coaches running to or via Colchester from London, the most famous being the Norwich Mail, which left London at 8p.m., hurtled post-haste through the night and reached Colchester at 2.40a.m.

And yet, apart from a brief revival in 1890, the last coach service, the gloriously named *Golden Path*, was discontinued only five years later in November 1843. Both the Hythe's trade and the stagecoach had been dealt a shattering blow by the same force. The railway.

Colchester station's gestation period was seven years. The eastern Counties Railway was incorporated on July 4th, 1836 with the avowed intent to provide a railway 126 miles long from Shoreditch to Great Yarmouth via Colchester, Ipswich and Norwich. After some bitter arguments over funding and then over the guage to which the railway was to be built, construction began late in March 1837.

The construction became bogged down both literally and metaphorically. Firstly the marshes near Stratford brought unexpected engineering problems and then lengthy wrangles followed with landowners reluctant to part with their land for less than somewhat more than the going rate. More engineering difficulties occurred when severe rain in 1841 damaged the earthworks and caused subsidence at Kelvedon and Mountnessing. The final section of the line from Brentwood to Colchester was eventually opened for passenger traffic on March 29th, 1843. An official reception was laid on and many of the town's dignitaries waited on the platform for the first train to arrive. It was a vain wait. The first train was two days late. This will come as no surprise at all to present day commuters on the Colchester-London line.

When the train did eventually arrive the official party whisked their visitors off by foot for a celebration at the Three Cups in the High Street. A band played at the head of the procession and church bells pealed out. It makes you feel like that when the train is actually on time.

So much time and money had been spent on the effort of reaching Colchester that the Directors of the Eastern Counties Railway promptly cancelled plans to continue any further, much to the annoyance of the inhabitants of Ipswich and Norwich.

Eventually a new company, the Eastern Union built a railway between Colchester and Ipswich but as the two companies were bitter enemies they could come to no satisfactory arrangements regarding through running from Ipswich to London. The Eastern Counties either laid on very slow London trains to meet the Ipswich one or none at all. The circumstances were also such that the layout of tracks to Colchester station were very awkward and when the two companies merged it left the legacy for many years of the very tight curve at the station which caused through trains to slow down considerably.

On April 1st, 1849 a connection to the Hythe was built and on March 1st, 1866 the line to St. Botolph's was completed. This short spur eventually became very important for freight traffic and during the first World War as an embarkation point for soldiers from Colchester garrison.

The Great Eastern Railway station at Colchester in the Edwardian period showing the curve, a legacy of the bitter rivalry between the Eastern Counties and the Eastern Union Railway.

The line into Tendring was extended to Walton in 1867 and to Clacton in 1882, Harwich having already been reached in 1854.

Colchester station rapidly became an important centre and played a major part in the economic expansion of the town just as it has done in more recent years with regard to population expansion. After the second World War especially, many people who worked in London were attracted to the area by cheap house prices and the (potentially) rapid link with London. This process speeded up after full electrification of the line came about on June 17th, 1963.

The station itself received its first refreshment facilities in 1854, was almost totally rebuilt in 1865 and the track straightened out when electrification came in. For many years Colchester station appeared in the *Guiness Book of Records* as having the longest platform in Britain, but it has recently been demoted to second place, the 'Championship' now going to Gloucester.

Colchester's other two stations have not fared so well. The Hythe now no longer serves the port and is just a suburban station serving the East End of town and St. Botolph's has lost its important position as the freight centre, though it is still well-used by passenger traffic because of its proximity to the Town Centre.

Colchester has only suffered one major rail disaster in its history. This occurred on July 12th, 1913 when the Cromer to London express crashed into a light engine just outside the station. Driver Barnard and Fireman Keeble were killed outright, Guard Burdett died on his way to the hospital.

Colchester's bus service evolved from the mid-nineteenth century Carrier Cart services operated by such people as:

JAMES GREENLEAF of West Mersea. By 1848 he was operating a thrice weekly service which eventually passed to Underwood's and was absorbed by Eastern National in 1935.

ARTHUR HUNWICK of Coggeshall, whose family had been operating on the Coggeshall to Colchester road since 1848.

PECK BROTHERS of East Bergholt who had worked the East Bergholt to Colchester road since the 1840s.

MOORE BROTHERS of Kelvedon, reputed to be the longest established business in the public passenger field to be run by the same family. They began in 1815 and served the Kelvedon to Colchester route twice weekly. They eventually went out of business in 1963 for the sole reason that there were no Moores no more.

By the 1880s there were just over 60 local carrier services running to, as well as those above, villages such as Wivenhoe, Nayland and Tollesbury.

1888 saw the first properly timetabled horse-bus service to run in Colchester. This was operated by A. W. Berry and Sons who ran from West Mersea to Colchester. They also had the distinction of running the first public motor bus in the area when they ran a Daimler Motor Wagonette on the same route in 1899. Berry's continued for some time and in 1905 they faced their first motorised competition when the Great Eastern Railway started running buses on exactly the same route. Following the agreement by Berry's to maintain a service to connect with trains, G.E.R. withdrew their competition on February 27th 1909.

Berry's eventually offered excursions and tours from an office at Scheregate where they also had a parcels depot. In their later years the fleet had a brown livery.

Until 1904, however, there was no sort of service inside Colchester itself. All the services were operating between Colchester and nearby towns and villages. The nearest anyone had come to this was firstly when a steam tramway system was proposed in 1884 to run from North Station to High Street and secondly when the British Electric Traction Co. Ltd. sought powers to operate trams on five routes. The first scheme folded through lack of cash after some track as far as Middleborough had actually been laid and the second proposal was rejected in favour of Colchester Corporation operating its own system.

And so it was that on July 28th, 1904, Colchester's tramway system was opened with due pomp and ceremony by the Mayoress who drove the first tram herself from the Town Hall to Lexden on to North Station and then back to the Town Hall.

The fleet consisted of sixteen trams operating three routes (North Station to Lexden, North Station to East Gates and North Station to Hythe) at fifteen minute intervals. In July 1906 a new route was opened to the Recreation Ground and two new trams were brought in. It cost a penny to travel to the end of the line except to Lexden which cost twopence.

Although fondly remembered by those with good and long memories as powerful and friendly vehicles gliding gracefully through the town's thoroughfares, there were times when they proved to be somewhat clumsy and unwieldly. On one occasion, for example, one caught the corner of a fruiterer's cart and sent his fruit flying down the street. On another occasion a tram jumped the rails and slid into the gutter. Two other trams had to haul it back on to the rails. (Many were the children late home from school through watching this local drama!)

◀ Colchester's one railway disaster occurred at 3.00p.m. on the afternoon of July 12th, 1913. As well as the three railwaymen who were killed, several passengers were injured. Much of the Cromer to London Express was smashed on impact. Amazingly the small light engine remained upright on the track.

Cheeses being unloaded from an LNER carrier cart at the rear of Oliver and Parker Grocers, 1a Head Street, in the mid 1920s.

One of the best vantage points for keen tram-watchers was the top of North Hill where a man was posted to change the points and the overhead wires. When he was not on duty the driver had to change the points, while the conductor jumped off to change the wires. Speeds were restricted to 12 m.p.h. generally but to only 6 m.p.h. in Crouch Street and down North Hill to just 4 m.p.h.

The trams carried twenty-two passengers inside and twenty-six outside on wooden slatted seats with backs that you flipped over at the end of the route so that they were facing the right way for the return.

Eventually their slowness and their inflexibility led the Corporation to abandon trams and on May 21st, 1928 the trams on the East Gates route were replaced by buses. These were followed by the other routes until the sad day finally came on December 9th, 1929, when Colchester's very last trams ran on the Recreation Ground and Hythe routes. What was even sadder was that not one of Colchester's fleet of trams was preserved intact. Some were scrapped, most were sold to a builder for site huts while others became garden sheds. A sorry end for the once proud tuscan and cream leviathans.

Following the demise of the trams, Colchester Corporation expanded its bus routes. By now most of the external routes were being operated by the National Omnibus and Transport Company which had moved into Colchester in 1914, gradually buying up local carriers as they progressed, although two long-established companies managed to come to amicable working arrangements with National and still, to this day, operate local services, namely Norfolk's of Nayland and Hedingham Omnibuses.

As well as normal bus services National commenced a theatre service in 1924 with one of their new fourteen-seat Chevrolets — their first buses to be fitted with pneumatic tyres. For a return fare of ten shillings and sixpence, you could be taken to the London *Alhambra* and provided with a reserved front row dress circle seat. On the way you could listen to a radio concert through specially equipped wireless headphones. The electrical installation was carried out by Joslin's of High Street.

On February 28th, 1929 the old National company split up and the Eastern National Company came into being. By then they were running bus routes from Colchester to Chelmsford, Harwich, Stoke-by-Nayland, Sudbury, Dedham, Halstead, Maldon, Clacton, Manningtree and Bures and Colchester had become a main centre of operations for Eastern National. They owned properties in Queen Street (garage and depot) and St. John's Street (enquiry and parcels office).

When Eastern National bought up Underwood's blue and cream saloon omnibuses in 1935 they took with it their three routes — from Colchester to West Mersea; West Mersea to East Mersea and Colchester to Fingringhoe. The new licence carried the odd condition that "any passengers, on arrival at the Bus Park, Colchester, could demand conveyance to the North Railway Station for a fare of fourpence so long as they had boarded prior to reaching the municipal boundary".

Meanwhile the Colchester Corporation had also been expanding its services and new routes were gradually introduced. By January 1933 there were seven routes altogether and in June of that year they introduced their first circular route

Wright's
IND COOPES
LEXDEN
YW 6481

ENTRANCE TO
LOCKE'S

◀ Between 1928 and 1929 Colchester's trams were withdrawn and replaced by buses. Here the old and new rest side by side at the junction of Bergholt and Nayland Roads. The building is the *Railway Hotel*, behind which the fish, destined for Colchester's shops, was auctioned at the beginning of the Second World War. The hotel is no more, the site having been covered by an enormous roundabout.

from High Street via Ipswich Road, along the by-pass to Lexden and back to High Street along Lexden Road. At first it only operated on Thursdays, Saturdays and Sunday afternoons.

By the outbreak of the Second World War both Eastern National and Colchester Corportion were thriving concerns, the former running the external routes from Colchester to local villages, the latter operating the internal routes. Some of the independent bus companies taken over by Eastern National included Jones & Harris of Rowhedge, Primrose Bus Service of West Mersea, The Transit Bus of Mile End, and C N Warner of Rowhedge.

After the war further expansion took place. Colchester Corporation laid on further routes to cope with the new housing estates and commuter traffic to North Station. Eastern National bought up more local companies including George Digby of Wormingford and Mawdsley and Brown of Rowhedge.

In 1959, Colchester Borough Transport completely reorganised their services and operated ten routes. These were soon followed by two others to the Greenstead and Barnhill Estates. Fares remained fairly stable throughout the 1950s and early 1960s. The fare from Head Street to North Station according to the 1954 timetable for example was twopence. By 1964 this had only risen to threepence. (Ironically though, the timetable itself had gone up from a penny to ninepence!).

In 1961 Eastern National offered their first route to actually cross Colchester when they ran through from Wormingford to Rowhedge.

Gradually traffic fell off as more people began to use private cars to get around and both Colchester Borough Transport and Eastern National had to rationalise their routes, in some cases by using the expedient of joint operation. Colchester Borough Transport also began bringing in special services to place such as Colchester Zoo on summer Sundays and, in 1979, a sightseeing tour of Colchester. Out-of-town shopping developments, such as High Woods, also created the need for new bus services.

◀ There was no hurry to dig up the tram lines. Some, like these in Queen Street, were dug up almost immediately but most lingered on until the second World War when they were dug up for scrap. Some even lasted until the 1950s.

Today both the CBT and Eastern National, though not carrying the traffic they once did, are still vital communication links for the people of Colchester.

Before leaving the subject of transport it should be noted that the first aeroplane to be seen in Colchester was M. Salmet's flying machine. He had taken off from Northampton (86 miles away) and landed on the golf links in Bergholt Road after a flight of one hour and five minutes. The date, August 1st, 1912.

And finally the first motor car in Colchester belonged to Doctor Laver. He took possession of his new-fangled contraption in 1896. Little did the good doctor, or those first gawping bystanders, realise what this invention would mean for the future of Colchester!

A Leyland Massey 61-seater belonging to Colchester Borough Transport hard at work in Crouch Street on June 2nd, 1973. Introduced in 1966, this particular bus lasted until 1978 and the type until 1980.

◀ An Eastern National Bristol K5G built in 1950 at rest in Colchester Bus Station during the 1950s. The bus pictured was, in fact, the last of its type to be built for Eastern National.

The *Hippodrome* in its heyday as a music hall, just before the First World War. Its original name the *Grand Theatre* is still discernible in the roof. On the right is the *Lamb* Hotel, now known as the *Bay and Saye.*

Entertainment and Sport

The *Theatre Royal* was built in 1812 in Queen Street at a cost of £3000. Prices were, Boxes four shillings, Pit two shillings and Gallery one shilling. The first two plays to be put on were *A Touch of the Times* and *How to Die for Love* on November 2nd of that year. Following a somewhat difficult time, the theatre emerged into the 1880s under new management and with a wide variety of entertainments. As well as the professional theatre there were amateur performances, concerts and readings. So popular had the theatre become that performances began to take place at other halls in and around Colchester; there was the New Corn Exchange which started putting on shows in the Spring of 1884 and the Drill Hall in Stanwell Street which took away some of the amateur theatricals.

There was a severe blow to the *Theatre Royal* in 1887 when the magistrates refused to renew its licence on the grounds that it was unsafe in the event of a fire. After a number of alterations the licence was eventually restored in 1888.

Further improvements took place in 1901 when electric light and central heating were installed. During the Edwardian period attendances were generally poor, most people now preferring the Music Hall at the *Hippodrome* which had recently opened in the High Street. The only occasions when the Theatre became packed were when one of George Edwardes' companies visited Colchester and put on such well-known musicals as *The Quaker Girl* or *The Merry Widow.* Unfortunately George Edwardes was able to command such a high percentage of the takings that even with house-full notices out profits were very slight. Perhaps the most outstanding performance of this period came when Ellen Terry starred in George Bernard Shaw's *Captain Brassbound's Conversion.* Other star names to appear at the *Theatre Royal* included the Jersey Lily, Lily Langtree; Mrs Patrick Campbell and the seventeen year old Gladys Cooper who made her professional stage debut as *Bluebell in Fairyland* on December 18th, 1905. She earned £3 a week and was complimented by the *Essex Telegraph* as a "talented actress with a beautiful voice."

Such was the competition from the *Hippodrome* that in 1910 the *Theatre Royal* began putting on variety shows and in 1913 even dabbled with the new art form — the cinema.

The end came for the *Theatre Royal* on September 5th, 1918, when, at 1.25a.m. fire was reported to be burning inside the theatre. There was no hope. The building was completely destroyed. Ironically the Captain of Colchester Fire

Brigade, Mr Cocker, had been in the audience the night before to watch the last ever performance.

The theatre that had eclipsed the *Theatre Royal* started life on April 24th, 1905, as the *Grand Theatre.* In October the name was changed to the *Grand Palace of Varieties* and was then taken over by Walter de Frece, who owned a string of theatres around the country all called the *Hippodrome.* Consequently the *Grand* was, once again, renamed, and variety became the order of the day. During that halcyon period for the Music Hall, many stars passed through the *Hippodrome*'s narrow stage and dressing room doors beneath the overhanging gas lamps to tread carefully down the stone steps and out on to the stage. The delighted and enraptured audience meanwhile had entered the plush velvet auditorium through a much grander entrance passing the liveried doorman on their way in. Names such as Marie Lloyd, Harry Champion, Bransby Williams, George Formby Senior and Little Tich (who actually made his stage debut in Colchester in 1883 at the Sir Colin Campbell Music Hall in the Mersea Road) all did their bit. And in September 1912, a young man appeared on the bill as a member of the Fred Karno Company. A short while later he was to give up the British Music Hall for the lure of Holywood. His name — Charlie Chaplin. At this time many halls put on one-night stands and many famous names appeared at various venues. The Corn Exchange especially drew some of the period's leading stars — including Dan Leno, Jan Kubelik and Buffalo Bill.

With the demise of the Music Hall after the First World War, the *Hippodrome* went over to showing films — including a good number by that same Charlie Chaplin.

The next important date for Colchester's theatre was 1937, the year that Robert Digby and Beatrice Radley founded the Colchester Repertory Company in the *Albert Hall.* The 'Rep', as it came to be known, continued the tradition of putting on high-class professional plays in Colchester. A number of well-known actors made some of their earliest appearances at the *Albert Hall* as members of the Rep. Names such as Trevor Howard and Derek Bond spring to mind.

The Rep continued throughout the war, pausing only to go on tours arranged by E.N.S.A. After the war more well-known names appeared with the Company. In 1946, Anthony Newley made his stage debut at the age of fourteen and in 1949, Peggy Mount was a member of the Company.

The *Albert Hall* was never really a very suitable place for a theatre and almost from the beginning there was a campaign for a purpose-built theatre to be built. But it was not until 1970 that building finally began on a site within the shadow of Jumbo, and on May 10th, 1972, the *Mercury Theatre* opened, almost 54 years after the *Theatre Royal* had been burnt down.

Since then the *Mercury* has offered a variety of productions. Classical plays, modern plays, musicals and pantomimes have all been performed. The future of theatre in Colchester now seems assured and in the 1986/87 season 82% of all seats were sold.

During the '20s and '30s and even on into the '50s, the theatre had had to take a definite back seat to the cinema. The excitement of seeing your larger-than-life idol on the silver screen was considered almost worth risking life and limb for. At the *Headgate* it was said that two out of every three seats collapsed and at the

Vaudeville a big step down trapped the unwary and threw them to the floor with a frightful tumble.

The 'cinematograph' had first come to Colchester in the late nineteenth century, when visiting showmen set up their seemingly magical 'Bioscope' at the annual Colchester Fair. Twopence was all it cost to enter the darkened tent and watch in awe as shadowy figures paraded across a flickering screen.

Gradually public halls and theatres began showing the new moving pictures. The *Hippodrome*, for example, showed films as part of their variety programmes. But it was not until 1910 that buildings whose sole purpose was to show films began to appear and the cinema was born.

Colchester was quick off the mark when, on Wednesday November 30th, 1910, Grand Electric Empires Ltd. opened the *Electric Theatre*, Headgate, created out of the former lecture hall of the Liberal Club. The very first programme of films to be shown in a proper cinema in Colchester included *Scenes in the Valley of Bratland* and *Nellie's Farm* (the story of slum life in a large city). A gramaphone playing songs such as *Ship Ahoy* and *If I Should Plant a Tiny Seed of Love* ran synchronised to the films. Afternoon tea was served during the interval. The cinema ran continuous performances from 2.30p.m. to 11.00p.m.

In 1922 the cinema was sold to David Ager who renamed it the *Headgate*. It later changed its name to the *Cameo* and in 1967 became a branch of the National Film Theatre. It closed in 1976 to become a cycle shop.

Colchester's next cinema was the *Empire* in Mersea Road built by David Ager as the *Vaudeville* in 1911. Between the wars this became very famous for its Saturday Morning 'flicks'. A penny-a-time to see all your favourites — Laurel & Hardy, Harold Lloyd, Hoot Gibson, Buck Jones — and send you away to ponder all week how on earth Pearl White was going to escape from her latest predicament. The *Empire* closed in May 1959 and was demolished in 1971.

Broken Blossoms starring Lillian Gish and Richard Barthelmess and directed by D. W. Griffiths was the first film to be shown at the *Hippodrome* when it became a cinema in July 1920. It was later taken over by Gaumont and closed in 1961 when it 'sold out' to Bingo. The theatre was badly damaged by fire in 1972. It has recently been renovated as a night club while retaining as much of the old theatre as possible.

Colchester's last two cinemas to open were in complete contrast to the old 'flea pit' nature of the *Headgate* and the *Vaudeville* and both the *Playhouse* and the *Regal* were really swish affairs. The *Playhouse* in St. John's Street was built in 1928/29 and sold to Associated British Cinemas in 1932. In 1962 they spent £75,000 on a modernisation scheme and re-named it the A.B.C. Unfortunately it too has now become a bingo hall.

The *Regal*, Crouch Street, was opened on February 23rd, 1931, by Ager's Cinema Circuit Limited. It was designed by a cinema architect of national fame, Cecil Masey, who gave it a Spanish appearance and flavour. Just before the second World War it was acquired by Odeon Theatres. In 1974 the interior was completely restyled and turned into the *Odeon Film Centre* with three screens for patrons to choose from. The last to be built, the *Odeon* is the only cinema left in Colchester.

Outdoor recreation was — and is — also valued. The annual Colchester Fair, called to celebrate the oyster feast, at which moving pictures first appeared, was a very popular entertainment for many people. Other fairs were held at places such as Parson's Heath. Lexden Heath, Old Heath and the Hythe. In the nineteenth century an annual picnic was held for the 'poorer classes' at Lexden Springs. Bathing in the river was also popular, as were spectacles of any kind — the arrival of the railway, for example. For a whole month after its first arrival in Colchester crowds still flocked to the station to see the trains. The railway was also able to provide outings with cheap excursions to London proving a great success as did later excursions to the seaside.

In 1885 the Corporation leased the old parade ground of the earlier barracks and laid it out as a Recreation Ground. And in 1892 Wilson Marriage opened Castle Park to the public. Both of these open spaces have served several generations of Colcestrians wishing to relax, walk, play or listen to the band.

Over the last one-hundred years Colchester people have taken part, watched or gone to many forms of organised, self-organised or impromptu entertainments. Circuses, the Carnival, the Tattoo, Colchester Zoo and sports of all kind.

The *Headgate Cinema,* at the time of this photograph, still known as the *Electric Cinema,* is on the right and Fred Medcalf's Motorcycle shop on the left.

Colchester's two main parks. The Recreation Ground (above), formerly the old Garrison parade ground which was leased for public use by the Corporation in 1855 and the Castle Park opened in 1892 by Wilson Marriage.

Castle Park was used for many events, including this bicycle slow race held in 1923.

The elephants arrive for the circus (How many were called Jumbo?). Here they are ▶ marching down Crouch Street in the 1920s on their way to the Recreation Ground.

KING'S ARMS.

THE TAILSTOCK SEVEN
THE COLCHESTER LATHE COMPANY LIMITED
presents
THE TAILSTOCK SEVEN

◀ Amateur entertainment has been provided by many groups over the years. Here are Colchester Lathe Co.'s Tailstock Seven in 1963/4 on their way to the Carnival.

And, of course, no sport has been more popular than football. By the 1880s there were already a number of teams in action. Paxman's works side had started about 1873 to be followed by Colchester Town shortly afterwards. They first played at Land Lane and then hired the cricket club's ground at Cambridge Road. In the 1880s several other teams sprang up — the Excelsiors, the Crusaders and St. Peter's Institute. With the opening of six pitches on the Recreation Ground many more clubs came into being and by 1904, something like two-hundred and eighteen matches were played on the 'Rec.' during the season. At this time two of the leading clubs were Colchester Town and Colchester Crown, which must have been very confusing! Both played in the East Anglian League.

Most of the other leading clubs during the early years of this century were works teams and two of them Culver Street Iron Works (A. G. Mumford's) and Hythe Bridge Iron Works (Bracket's) won the Essex Junior League. One man who played for both teams was Wally Lawrence. He recalls that he started playing football with Magdalen Street School and then later helped to found the Artillery Street Club. Team meetings were held in a shed which normally housed a donkey. (The donkey was turned out before meetings!).

A number of the players from these teams went on to play for Colchester Town including George Dollimore, Fred Bloomfield and Orrie Pritchard. Wally left Hythe Bridge Iron Works team to join the Wimpole Road Weslyan team, who also won the Essex Junior Cup.

After the First World War Colchester Town Club, now playing at Layer Road, joined the Spartan League and were playing teams such as Wycombe Wanderers, Slough and G.E.R. Loughton. During the 1920s the club had close links with West Ham and players such as Benny and Ted Fenton turned out for Town.

In 1925, the Ipswich *Green'un* Newspaper started a series of ''Thumbnail Sketches of Famous Players''. Their first subject was Bill Dent, at that time captain of Bury Town, but later to become captain of Colchester. Bill remembers being paid four shillings travelling expenses for home matches as he lived at Lavenham and came in on his motor bike. Four shillings bought four gallons of petrol. There was great rivalry with Ipswich, who were in the Southern Amateur League, and Bill's proudest moment in football was when he captained Colchester to a 9–1 win over their great rivals.

In 1936 Ipswich turned professional and joined the Southern League. As a consequence the management of Colchester Town, now in the Essex Senior League, decided to start a professional club as well and so, in 1937, Colchester Utd. — The U's — was founded. Unfortunately in those days the Football Association frowned upon too much fraternisation between professional and amateur and ruled that the same management could not run both Colchester

◀ The show goes on! The 1988/89 pantomime at the*Mercury Theatre — Dick Whittington.*

The Culver Street Iron Works Team (A. G. Mumford's) in 1918/19, the year they won the Essex Junior Leageue.

Town and Colchester United. The management decided to stick by their new professional club. Town struggled on for another three months before finally folding in December 1937 when their players became United's reserve team.

Colchester United itself had been formed from players on Football League Club transfer lists. All were signed free. The first manager was Ted Davis, the former Huddersfield and Blackburn goalkeeper. The club joined the Southern League and were an overnight success winning the Southern League Cup in their first season and the League itself in 1938/39.

In the 1950/51 season the Football League extended the two Third Divisions (North & South) by four clubs and Colchester were elected to fill one of the places. Since that time the U's have never managed to get higher than Division Three. The nearest they came was in the 1956/57 season when they needed to win their last game to ensure promotion to Division Two. They lost. And as if that wasn't frustrating enough, the team promoted in their place was . . . Ipswich!

Nevertheless, Colchester have had some famous victories over the years, particularly in F.A. Cup matches. The most spectacular of all coming on the afternoon of February 13th, 1971, when goals from Simmons and Crawford (2) led to the U's defeating the mighty Leeds 3–2, at a time when Leeds were generally recognised as the best club in the country if not the whole of Europe.

A number of top players have passed through Colchester's books including Vic Keeble, Bobby Hunt, Kevin Beattie, Tony Macedo and John Bond. In all, at the time of writing, 309 players have turned out for the U's since they joined the Football League.

Colchester hold a number of League records (some more curious than others!):

- They were the first non-league club to reach the fifth round of the F.A. Cup – in 1947/48.
- They appeared in the first ever televised football match – against Wealdstone in 1948.
- Ron Meades became the manager with the shortest tenure in the Football League when he was appointed one Thursday during the 1952/53 season and was sacked on the following Sunday.
- Hal Mason, the club statistician, is currently the longest serving employee of any Football League club – 39 years.
- Graham Layzell is the longest serving first team coach driver in the football league. He has been driving Colchester's Osborne Coach to away matches for 21 years.

Other famous or well-remembered names associated with the club include Neil Franklin, the England international who was manager from 1963-68; Fred Draycott, who reported on Colchester's games (Town and United) for the Press Association between 1920 and 1950 and only missed six first team games. (He was succeeded by Hal Mason who has reported ever since and has himself only missed three!); Claude Orrin, the Club Secretary 1946-70, who built up the club after five years inactivity during the war and finally the two mascots Harry Fosker, the umbrella man, 1946-53 and Taffy (with his dog) 1956-70.

The U's are currently going through a somewhat depressed period. At the time of writing they are bottom of the Fourth Division and their average gates have dropped from a high of 10,000 in the early to mid '50s to an all-time low today of just about 2,000. In addition the Layer Road ground has been sold for housing development and will have to be vacated within the next two years.

On the brighter side a new manager and first team coach have just been named. Jock Wallace, formerly manager of Glasgow Rangers and Leicester City, becomes the fourteenth full-time manager since the club was founded in 1937, while the former England world cup star Alan Ball has been appointed coach.

It is also worthy of note that in the 1987/88 season Colchester was the only club in the whole of the Football League not to have anyone arrested inside the ground.

Just as a footnote – in the 1938-39 season Colchester paid the total sum of £5 15s for police services.

The first recorded cricket match in Colchester took place in 1749 when a Colchester side played a combined Manningtree and Brightlingsea team at the *Sign of the Fencers* in Tenant's Lane, Colchester. Two years later Manningtree and Brightlingsea again combined to play the parishes of St. Nicholas and St. Botolph's. In the same year Colchester advertised that they would play "any eleven for 11 black velvet caps; to meet at the Sign of the Pig at Botolph's gate; a Sixpenny Ordinary provided".

By 1800, the Colchester side seems to have been fairly well-established, though they were routed by the Herts Militia in a match on Lexden Heath in that year.

In 1864-65 an all Essex County Club was formed and, in consequence of the Colchester and East Essex Club having obtained land at Wimpole Lane to play their matches, the County Club agreed to make their home there also. In August 1866 Essex beat Surrey on this ground by an innings and 171 runs. Unfortunately at the end of this season the Essex Club folded up.

The Colchester & East Essex Club on the other hand went from strength to strength and by the turn of the century was playing at Cambridge Road. In 1908 the Club moved to Castle Park where it has remained ever since. The first century scored on the ground was by B. H. Kent. A number of the club members have gone on to play for the Essex First XI, including D. C. Robinson, E. S. Missen, H. P. Waugh and F. W. H. Nicholas.

The Colchester squad for the famous cup tie against Leeds on February 13th, 1971. As well as the goal scorers, Simmons and Crawford, the other hero of the match was the goalkeeper, Graham Smith, who pulled off a spectacular save just two minutes from the end, thus ensuring victory for the "U's".

Meanwhile the Essex County Club had reformed in 1876 and in 1894 was granted first-class status. But it was not until June 18th, 1914, that they returned to play at Colchester on Castle Park, where they beat Worcestershire by 193 runs. World War I interrupted Essex cricket and it was another six years before they came back to Colchester as part of their policy of playing at different grounds throughout the County during the season. The venue chosen was the Garrison Ground, where they lost both matches by an innings — to Hampshire and Glocestershire. They continued to play at the Garrison Ground until poor attendances in the late '20s and early '30s led to Essex issuing a statement in 1932 that they would no longer be playing matches at Colchester. However, two years later Essex were back and back to the Castle Park Ground, where they have held their Colchester week ever since.

Some of the outstanding performances seen at Colchester over the years have included a third wicket partnership of 333 between R. M. Taylor & J. O'Connor against Northamptonshire in 1937; a score of 219 not out by Doug Insole against Yorkshire in 1949; 16 wickets taken by T. P. B. Smith in the match against Middlesex in 1947 and 7 catches taken by wicketkeeper Brian Taylor in two matches, v. Kent in 1961 and against Gloucestershire in 1964.

The first ever Rugby match to be played in Colchester was played between the Colchester and East Essex Cricket Club (!) and the Garrison about 1870 but it was not until 1925 that the Colchester Rugby Club was founded. Although starting off with eleven wins out of nineteen matches and fielding two teams, one on Saturday, the other on Thursday, it was felt necessary to suspend the club for lack of support at the 1927 A.G.M. The Thursday fixture list was taken over personally by the Club Secretary, Norman Pertwee, and the club continued as N. F. Pertwee's XV. On September 20th, 1928, the Colchester Rugby Club was re-formed and took back N. F. Pertwee's XV's fixtures, while he was elected captain and secretary.

The team played as guests of the Army at Reed Hall, occasionally using the *Red Lion,* High Street, as changing rooms. The club then moved to Lexden Show Ground and moved their changing rooms to *The Cups,* also in the High Street. The club played some of the region's leading teams before the war including Ipswich, Clacton, Upper Clapton and St. John's College, Cambridge and always managed to impress if not actually win.

After the war the club built its first clubhouse at Mile End in September 1953 and moved to its present premises in Mill Road on October 1st, 1978, with a match against Eastern Counties. The official opening ceremony was performed by former England international and television commentator, Nigel Starmer-Smith.

Some of the best players to have played for Colchester include internationals Jim Unwin, Boy Withers and Rees Jones.

Another popular team game has recently been introduced to Colchester with the formation of the Colchester Gladiators American Football Team in 1983. Attendances for the Budweiser Premier League outfit average around the 700 mark and in the 1987/88 season the team maintained a 100 per cent winning record clinching the London North and East divisional title.

In May 1878, the Colchester & East Essex Lawn Tennis Club opened its new courts at Cambridge Road. In August 1889, a tournament open to players in the Eastern Counties was held and received about ninety entries. This event became an annual fixture. The courts do not appear to have been that brilliant however, as in a book *My Tournaments* published in 1922, F. N. Burrow said that they were ''some of the worst provided on a dusty day. I have known play stopped for a minute or two because of the clouds of dust. If, however, it rained, they were slippery, being full of clover''.

Paxman's Athletics Club began their annual sports day in 1915 and by 1925 it was firmly established as the premier athletic event of the year.

Bill Dent, Colchester's best ever athlete at the peak of his career, with just a few of his many trophies.

Bill Dent (the Colchester Town Fooball Captain) was the star performer at these events throughout the 1920s. At one time he was tipped to make the British team for the Los Angeles Olympics of 1932 in the 120 yards hurdles following his brilliant run in the Inter-Counties Championship of 1931 when he came third to Lord Burleigh. Unfortunately he was injured at football and was unable to go. Sadly his athletics career more or less came to an end while he was still at his peak when he contracted diptheria in 1934

Before leaving sport in Colchester mention must also be made of Alf Medcalf, whose father, Fred Medcalf, owned a motor cycle shop at Headgate. Alf was brought up surrounded by names such as Triumph, Rudge, Whitworth and Douglas and as soon as he could he joined the Colchester Motor Cycle Club. He would practice for hours on end on his 'Duggie' on the Lowestoft sea front and by the early 1920s was one of the region's leading racers and hill-climbers, for which he used an old belt-driven Norton.

On February 19th, 1928, the first ever speedway meeting, organised jointly by the Ilford and Colchester Motor Cycle Clubs, was staged in this country at High Beech near Loughton. Alf took his Douglas along to see what it was all about. On arrival he found that he had been programmed to take part in the very first race of that very first meeting. Alf went on to win the race thereby inscribing his name in the récord books for all time. He was also presented with a cup at the end of the day which read ''Awarded for the fastest lap – First British Dirt Track Races – High Beech, 19th February 1928''. This was to remain Alf's most prized possession.

He later went on to ride in the first ever meetings at Harringay, Wimbledon and White City. At the White City in one race his bike burst into flames only twenty yards from the finishing line but he managed to push it home to take third place. His career ended when he broke his leg in a bad fall, also at White City, and decided to call it a day.

One of the posters advertising the Pageant. Note the prices.

Colchester Pageant

In the entertainment field there can be no doubt that Colchester's major event of the last hundred years was the Pageant of 1909. The playwright Louis Napoleon Parker had invented the modern pageant — the idea of a spectacular presentation of a town's history — in the early years of the century. His first four at Sherborne, Warwick, Bury St. Edmunds and Dover met with enormous acclaim and success. As 'Britain's Oldest Recorded Town' it was little wonder that Colchester, under the leadership of the Mayor, Cllr. W. Gurney Benham and the Deputy-Mayor, Alderman Wilson Marriage, should ask Mr. Parker to produce a pageant for them.

Because of the success of his other Pageants, Mr. Parker was much in demand and had had numerous requests to produce Pageants all over Britain, but he was so impressed with Colchester's unique historical record that he agreed to perform the task.

A Colchester Pageant Committee was set up under the Presidency of the Earl of Warwick, Lord Lieutenant of the County, and the Town Council placed part of Castle Park at the Committee's disposal. For two years, Mr. Parker and the Committee worked to get the presentation just right. Over three thousand performers were involved and practically all their costumes were made by voluntary helpers.

On the piece of ground chosen — near the lake at the bottom of Castle Hill — a temple with white columns was erected directly facing the grandstand while entrances and exits were erected on each side.

The Pageant itself told the story of Colchester and ran as a continuous performance without intervals. It was written by Mr. Parker, with contributions from W. Gurney Benham and C. E. Benham.

Episode one started with a dialogue between Kymbeline, Caradoc, Gwyddyr and other legendary figures, and the discovery that the oyster was edible. This first oyster feast was interrupted by the Romans, when in a particularly fine scene, Claudius was shown arriving in his chariot with soldiers, trumpeters and singing and dancing girls. This scene in its turn was interrupted by Boadicea and her troop of Iceni and was followed by King Coel and his daughter Helena arriving.

◀ A procession through Colchester advertising the Pageant.

Episode two moved on to Saxon times and included the story of Osyth and the invasion by the Danes.

The third episode was highly spectacular and particularly well-dressed and took Colchester through the Middle Ages, including the granting of the Charter by King Richard I in 1189. The episode came to an end with a gorgeous procession of mounted men and ladies following King Henry VI.

The next episode matched the previous one for colour and richness when Queen Elizabeth I appeared on a pie-bald steed surrounded by her gloriously costumed nobles.

The happy atmosphere of the Tudor Court gave way in the next episode to the privations of the Siege of 1648 with some very dramatic moments as volleys of musketry were heard in the distance getting closer and closer and then the climax of the scene with the execution of Lucas and Lisle.

The final tableau was extremely effective with the Royal Grammar School *Carmen*, written by the Headmaster Mr. P. Shaw Jeffrey, sung by the full chorus. During this Triumph Song the entire mass of performers assembled and finally marched away. A few days later all the props were sold off by public auction.

Contemporary criticism of the Pageant points to there being too much dialogue in certain places and not enough action and that, in any case, much of the conversation was inaudible. However, there was very high praise for the colour, the grouping, the dress, the crowd scenes and the spectacular effects of the dances and set pieces.

In all, the Pageant was considered an outstanding success and is still remembered vividly by the few remaining Colcestrians who were actually there.

Colchester Pageant
Emperor Claudius and Retinue

Volunteers hard at work erecting the stand for the Pageant while bystanders get a free view during a rehearsal. Over fifty thousand people were eventually to watch the Pageant.

Part of the Final Tableau, with the whole cast singing the *Royal Grammar School Carmen.*

◀ One of the Pageant's most spectacular scenes — the Emperor Claudius and his Retinue.

Staff and pupils at the short-lived Lexden Quaker School in the 1890s.

Pupils at the Canterbury Road School in 1912.

Schools and Colleges

By the 1880s Colchester schools had reached crisis point. The 1870 Education Act had made it compulsory for all children of school-going age to be taught by trained teachers in a satisfactory school building and had laid down that a School Board should be publicly elected and a survey made of the current educational provision. In Colchester this survey revealed that about half the existing schools were not satisfactory and that, in any case, there were not enough places being provided. The Chairman of the School Attendance Committee was concerned that something like a thousand children in Colchester were getting no formal education of any kind. Consequently, in the 1890s, a huge school building programme was put into effect. North Street and Old Heath opened in 1895, Barrack Street in 1896, St. John's Green in 1897 and Stockwell Street in 1898.

The transfer of authority for education from the School Board to the Borough in 1902 did nothing to stop the vigorous building programme and Canterbury Road followed in 1903, Mile End in 1906 and East Ward in 1908.

Some of the better older non-Board schools continued in existence. One, in particular, the Culver Street Weslyan School, received several accolades during this period. In 1884 the Board of Education named it as one of the best four schools in the whole of Essex and in 1890 it received the maximum possible grant for its success in the annual examination. The headmaster during this period was Henry Shaw who retired in 1916 after forty-five years as Head.

Other well-known headmasters of the pre-First World War era included John Harper, the Headmaster at North Street School and John Cheese at St. John's Green. Although school discipline was somewhat harder in those days there was a happy atmosphere at most Colchester schools and there are still many fond memories of those 'happiest days of our lives'. Jack Gomer remembers well for example, the 1911 Coronation of George V when the whole school boarded the trams and headed for the Coronation Tea at the Recreation Ground. He also remembers that discipline wasn't so much hard as arbitrary in some cases. One teacher at St. John's Road used to line up anyone who misbehaved in the playground in front of the class and told them to hold out their hand. He'd then move down the line saying, "Is this one saucy?", to which he would give his own answer, either "yes" or "no". If the answer was 'yes' he would administer a severe blow with the cane on the hand, if the answer was 'no' it would just be a slight tap. Jack says he could never see any real reason why some should have been "yes" and others "no".

The question of discipline also exercised the mind of John Cheese over at St. John's Green. In the log book dated September 12th, 1898, he wrote: —"I have decided to allow all certificated teachers the use of the cane in their classrooms — provided it be used with discretion and for trivial offences in class only''!

The Headmaster at Barrack Street School, Edward North, had, however, come to a different method of working when he decreed, in 1901, that there would be just one cane in the school — on his desk.

If life wasn't too bad for the pupils it wasn't all that good for trainee teachers. Formal teacher training was virtually non-existent. On leaving school, a trainee would become a pupil-teacher taking his lessons at 6.30a.m. and then taking classes all day, some of which consisted of over ninety children. In the evening he was expected to devote himself to study.

Schools continued during the First World War without too much interruption though there was an unfortunate incident at St. John's Green when the headmaster was assaulted by an irate woman demanding her children be allowed home as there was an air-raid on. The magistrates agreed with the headmaster that the safest place for the children was at school and bound the woman over for twelve months and ordered her to pay eight shillings costs. The prosecuting counsel remarked that it ''might be useful if all schools were placed on the telephone''.

After the First World War the smell of chalk on slates gradually gave way to the inkwell, ink blots and ink pellets. In 1920, the Culver Street Weslyan Day School was forced to close and the school assembled for the last time on 27th July of that year. The headmaster was presented with a pair of silver-mounted hair brushes. Most of the pupils were transferred to the newly opened Hamilton Road school.

During the 1920s and '30s sports became a very important part of the curriculum and there was much inter-school rivalry. The Annual Schools Sports day was held on Paxman's Athletics Ground at Land Lane and the Markham Cup Final (for football) at Layer Road. The Barrack Street School had a particularly fine team in the 1920s and in 1923 won the cup final by beating St. John's Green 9-0. The team included Keeble who later played for Essex schoolboys.

In 1934, the Milk Marketing Board began its Free Milk scheme and all schools in the area received their quota of third-pint bottles of milk. And so the busy life of the milk monitor began.....

Just before war broke out in September 1939, evacuees began arriving from London. Emergency rations which had been provided to schools were taken out of their hiding places and got ready. The first two trainloads of evacuees arrived at St. Botolph's on 1st September at 10.00a.m. On arriving at the various schools they were given biscuits and tea, coffee or milk. They were then given emergency rations for 48 hours and driven round Colchester and surrounding villages looking for billets. In the weeks to come shop keepers became very accustomed to changing the shilling postal orders sent from home to the evacuees.

Although supposed to carry a gas mask at all times most children would throw them into a corner at playtime or use them as improvised toys swinging them in a circle while making the noise of an aeroplane! Most children also carried small boxes containing some food intended as use for emergency rations in case of a prolonged air-raid.

It wasn't long before the evacuees started going in the opposite direction and parties of Colchester school children headed for Kettering, Stoke-on-Trent and Wellingborough. At the Wilson Marriage School only seventy-six pupils were left out of the two-hundred plus registered before the war. It was a similar story in the other schools.

For those left at school there was considerable disruption due to air-raids and hours of attendance were reduced. As the war continued the numbers of evacuees returning rose dramatically much to the annoyance of the authorities but much to the delight of the parents.

In 1944 a group of school children were entertained by fifty American soldiers. Included in the entertainment was ice cream, an unheard of luxury during the war.

Following the war things settled down quite quickly in Colchester's schools. In the 1950s schools began organising more out-of-hours and holiday activities, the most popular being trips firstly in this country and then abroad.

In 1972 a big reorganisation took place when the comprehensive system came in. Although schools modernised with ever more sophisticated equipment in the form of new science laboratories, computers and so on, the same spirit still pervaded the schools as it had always done. Many of Colchester's 'Board Schools' are now approaching their centenary and looking forward to an even better future.

Colchester is one of the few places in the country to retain selective education. The County High School for Girls was founded in 1909 under the title County Secondary School. It began with classrooms on the first floor of the Albert Hall in the High Street. In 1912 accommodation became available in the new Technical College on North Hill. The school colours were blue and silver and it was a school rule that every girl was expected to wear the school cap, or 'a sailor hat with the school hat band'.

By 1920 there were four-hundred pupils at the school and there was serious overcrowding. Consequently Greyfriars was bought and adapted for use by the juniors. During the inter-war years the school continued to expand and many out-of-school activities started such as an Historical and Archaeological Society, a Debating Circle, folk-dancing, brass-rubbing and play readings. Academic achievement was very high and large numbers went on to University.

The school continued its high standards after the war. In 1953 the County High School became the first school in the country to introduce micro-chemistry. In 1957 both parts of the school moved into new buildings at Norman Way where it has remained ever since.

Further and higher education in Colchester had its beginnings in the nineteenth century with the Mechanics' Institute, the Literary Institute, the YMCA and the Elementary District School of Art.

The industrial development of the 1880s brought a new urgency to the need for better education and in 1885, James Paxman brought together interested parties at a meeting in the Town Hall. From this meeting a committee was elected which then rented the Corn Exchange and adapted it for use as a college. Six months later the Albert School of Science and Art was born.

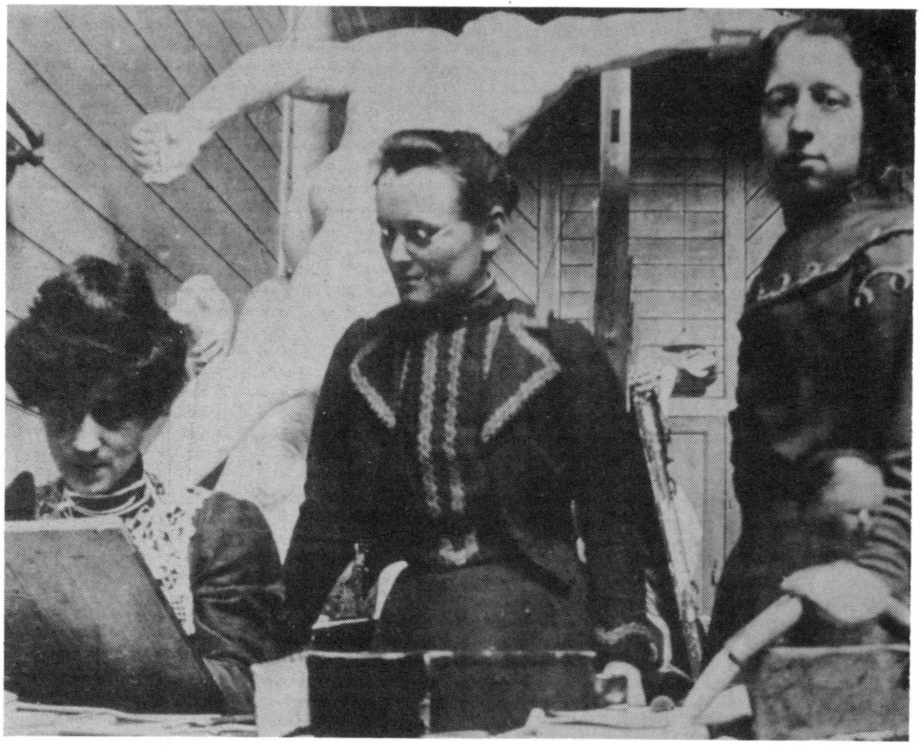

Students studying art and sculpture at the Old Albert Hall School of Art during the Edwardian period.

On 6th May, 1896, a report of the Town Council recommended the founding of the 'Colchester Technical and University Extension College' and the interior of the Old Corn Exchange, by now the property of the Council, was reconstructed and provided with class and lecture rooms and laboratories. The remodelled building was opened by the Earl of Rosebery on 20th October, 1896.

Even with the remodelling the accommodation rapidly became inadequate and it became necessary to plan a new college to provide technical education for the whole of North East Essex. The new building on North Hill was formally opened on 12th July, 1912. It housed the Art School, the Junior Trade School (forerunner of the County Technical School), the Pupil-Teachers' Training Centre and ran evening classes in technical, commercial and domestic subjects.

By the early 1950s, with the addition of the Department of Applied Sciences and the Commercial Department and the need to provide better laboratory and engineering facilities and machine workshops, the building once again became inadequate and yet another new home for the college went up in Sheepen Road.

Today the Colchester Institute, as it is now called, boasts eight-thousand students and a full-time staff of four-hundred and sixty. About twenty per cent of the students are pursuing higher education and the rest further education. The college now offers a music degree and Higher National Diplomas in industrial design, graphic design and hotel and catering studies.

Due to the continuing expansion it has once again become necessary to provide new buildings though this time they will be on the same site.

◀ By the mid-fifties a visit by a photographer to take individual and class photographs had become an annual event. Here in 1956 Class Four at Old Heath Primary School pose with their teacher, Mr. Farthing.

Colchester's newest and biggest educational establishment for further education was announced in the House of Commons on 18th May, 1961, by Mr. Selwyn Lloyd. On that day he told the House that four new universities were to be built, one of which would be at Colchester. The three sites originally looked at to house the University were the Kingsford area, 'near the Colchester Golf Club' and Wivenhoe Park. The news that it was to be Wivenhoe Park came on 9th November of the same year and on 19th January, 1962, the *Essex County Standard* announced that a contract had been completed for the sale of Wivenhoe Park from its owner, Mr. C. M. D. Gooch to Essex County Council for £175,000.

Professor A. E. Sloman was appointed Vice-Chancellor in July 1962, and the then Deputy Prime Minister, Mr. R. A. Butler, the Chancellor in October 1962. The University of Essex eventually opened on October 2nd, 1964 with one-hundred and twenty-two undergraduates.

Although there were some misgivings at first, the University has integrated well into the life of the community, and, just like the military garrison, has given a welcome boost to the town's trade. Today the University numbers three-thousand, one-hundred students and is firmly established as one of Britain's leading universities.

Sir Albert Sloman, newly appointed Vice Chancellor, walks round the site of the new University of Essex together with the Chancellor, R. A. Butler in 1962.

The Royal Grammar School

From one of Colchester's newest educational establishments to its oldest — the Colchester Royal Grammar School.

Nobody knows for sure just how old the School is. The earliest mention comes in 1206 when it is recorded that the Bishop of London held four acres of land in Colchester which included a school. In the Domesday Book, compiled in 1086, the Bishop is also shown to hold four acres on which there were fourteen buildings. Could one of those buildings have been the School?

The School is mentioned many times over the next three-hundred years, but the next major landmark came in 1584, when Queen Elizabeth I granted the School a Royal Charter and ordered that the house called Westons, ''which hath byn used to be a Grammar Schole .... shall be the free Grammar Schole''. Westons was situated in Culver Street.

The School continued in Culver Street until 1853, at which time it moved to a field between the Hospital and Beverley Lodge on the Lexden Road — its present site. The new school cost £3,500 and consisted of a school room (now the library) and two small classrooms (now the library annexe) as well as the dormitory and the Headmaster's house.

By the 1880s the influence of the school had declined owing to a long running controversy over its status and how it was to be funded. Although he tried his best, the Headmaster the Revd. Charles Acland, felt that he was getting nowhere and so resigned in 1892.

Following his resignation serious concern was expressed about the future of the school, until an order in Council in May 1899 cleared up, once and for all, the exact status of the school, establishing a governing body and placing the school under the control of the local authority.

In 1900 Mr. Percy Shaw Jeffrey was appointed headmaster and the school, free at last of the controversy that had dogged it for the past thirty years, entered into a golden era.

The number of pupils at the school had fallen to less than thirty, the buildings were filthy, there was no bathroom and the dormitory windows were nailed shut. In addition, hanging from the ceiling of the schoolroom were hundreds of penholder darts and even more blobs of chewed-up paper. Shaw Jeffrey had the schoolroom scrubbed five or six times before term began.

Throughout his tenure of office, Shaw Jeffrey worked unceasingly to raise the standards of the school both academically and materially and in 1910 the present hall plus three classrooms on the east side, two on the site of the present stage and a physics block were built and the Park Road playing fields purchased.

To the Grammar School boys, Percy Shaw Jeffrey inspired respect and admiration and inculcated a hatred of untidiness and slovenly behaviour.

He started the house system at the school with red caps for School House, blue caps for North Town and green caps for South Town. When he found that other schools in the town were copying his example and using the same colours he asked the school hatter what was the most expensive and difficult colour to get hold of. When he replied ''purple'', Shaw Jeffrey immediately made the school colours purple and gold and introduced badges for the different houses instead.

He loved mottoes and slogans and one of his favourites was 'Ride hard, shoot straight, hit from the shoulder and speak the truth'. To the rest of the staff he had vitality, originality and humour which he combined with firm but fair and consistent discipline. Percy Shaw Jeffrey retired in 1916 and was presented with a framed portrait by the school governors.

The new headmaster was Mr. H. J. Cape who continued Shaw Jeffrey's work of expanding the school. Elyanore House was acquired in 1920 and the swimming pool built in 1923 following a massive fund-raising event — a three-day 'Old English Fair' which raised the whole of the £1000 necessary.

Some of the teaching staff of this period were well-known as real characters — 'Daddy' Reeves, the chemistry master, who cleaned out test tubes with his gown; Mr. Saunders, with his *pince-nez;* Mr. Jones, who had an unerring aim with a piece of chalk; and the debonair Mr. Pepper, the English master. The old tuck shop selling cream slices is also well remembered!

In those years the Tudor Society flourished putting on concerts, with both masters and boys performing, while the Boarders' Party was an eargerly looked-forward-to feast when each boarder was allowed to invite one of his 'day-boy' friends. Mr. Soar did his conjuring tricks and Mr. Acheson — the 'country squire' — placed the threepenny bits in the pudding.

To encourage good work at school, 'Good Tickets' were given out to those who had performed satisfactorily. Recipients were allowed a free Saturday morning.

A big change came to the school in 1933 when pupils were admitted by annual scholarship and fee-paying was ended. Gurney Benham House (formerly Beverley Lodge) was purchased in 1934 and eventually became home for both the language and the chemistry laboratories as well as the boarders common rooms. In 1937 a new headmaster, Mr. A. W. Fletcher was appointed.

The war brought with it the 'Dig for Victory' vegetable plots near the indoor cricket school. Mr. Mabbs (or 'Mabbo') was the keen proponent of this idea. He also hated wasted food at lunch and, if he saw any left on the plate, would thunder ''which boy is wasting food that is precious?''. He would then rave on about 'Germans, Nazis, wasters and spies'', finishing with the curse 'You should starve to death, miserable boy''.

In the late 1940s, Mr. J. F. Elam became headmaster and Vic Keeble, the future Colchester, Newcastle and West Ham footballer, became School Captain. The school's pre-war tradition of magnificent Gilbert & Sullivan productions continued and inter-house competitions were still eagerly contested.

1964 saw major extensions to the school buildings with new chemistry laboratories, a new art and craft block, a canteen, a new stage and green room and an upper storey added to the classrooms alongside the Hall.

In 1968 Mr. Elam retired and Dr. S. Gardner was appointed Headmaster. The school leapt into yet another new era with electronics and computers well to the fore, and most amazing of all, soccer was reintroduced in 1979!

Dr. Gardner retired in 1984. His place being taken by the curent Headmaster, Mr. S. A. C. Francis, M.A.

The Old Colcestrian Society was founded by Shaw Jeffrey in 1901 and has flourished ever since. It has organised many fund raising events for the school and has been active in all aspects of the school's social life. It is a fitting tribute to the school that so many of its old boys still wish to remain associated with it through the Society.

The Programme cover for the Old English Fair held on May 31st, June 1st and 2nd, 1923, which raised over one thousand pounds for the new swimming pool.

1933-4

◀ The School in 1890. The Headmaster, the Revd. Charles Acland is standing on the right.

◀ The 1933-4 School Rugby Team. The Captain, Waller, is holding the ball.

Lord Rosebery opening the new buildings in 1910. Alongside Lord Rosebery on the platform are the Headmaster, Mr. P. Shaw Jeffrey (first on the left); the Mayor, Cllr. Alex Blaxhill (fifth from the left) and the Member of Parliament, Major L. Evans (seventh from the left). At the opening ceremony, Lord Rosebery declared "If you cannot breed men in Colchester, where are they to be bred?" Which seems as good a quotation as any on which to conclude this look back over Colchester's last one hundred years.

Floreat Colcestria!

Select Bibliography

GENERAL

BROWN, A. F. J. – *Colchester 1815-1914* (Essex County Council, 1980)
CANEY, Ella M. – *Remembering* (Dolphin Publications, 1986)
DOWDY, Mac. – *Colchester Town Trial* (Observations Unlimited, 1981)
GIFFORD, Philip – *Colchester As It Was* (Hendon Publishing, 1972)
GIFFORD, Philip – *Yesterday's Town: Colchester* (Barracuda Books, 1987)
MALING, J. J. – *Colchester Through The Ages* (East Anglia Magazine, 1984)
MARRIAGE, John – *Colchester A Pictorial History* (Philmore, 1988)
MARTIN, Geoffrey – *The Story Of Colchester From Roman Times To The Present Day* (Benham Newspapers, 1959)
McCALLUM, J. R. – *Colchester's Port — The Hythe And Its Church* (J. R. McCallum, 1947)
NEWMAN, Edward – *Memories Of A Bygone Age* (Photoprint, 1985)
PHILLIPS, Andrew – *Ten Men And Colchester* (Essex Record Office, 1985)
PLUCKWELL, George – *Colchester In Old Picture Postcards* (European Library, 1984)
SHERRY, Peter – *A Grand Old Town* (Dolphin Publications, 1987)
SHERRY, Peter – *A Portrait Of Victorian Colchester* (Egon Publishers, 1982)
STEPHENSON, David – *The Book Of Colchester* (Barracuda Books, 1978)

1880s

HAINING, Peter – *The Great English Earthquake* (Robert Hale, 1976)

WARTIME & MILITARY

COCKERILL, Chloe and WOODWARD, Daphne – *Colchester As A Military Centre* (Essex County Library, 1978)

SHOPS

BLAXILL, Nicholas – *A Family Firm In Colchester* (Kent, Blaxill, 1988)
CULLINGFORD & CO. LTD. – *History Of Cullingfords* (Cullingford & Co. Ltd., 1985)
LEWINGTON, Harry W. –
A Brief Historical Account Of The Colchester And East Essex Co-operative Society (Colchester & East Essex Co-op, 1977)
LONDON, David – *The Story Of Hatfields 1886-1986* (Hatfields, 1986)

OYSTERS & ROSES

BENHAM, W. Gurney – *Colchester Oyster Feast, Its History And Its Toast Lists* (Essex County Standard, 1902)

TRANSPORT

CRAWLEY, R. J., MACGREGOR, D. R. & SIMPSON, F. D. –
The Years Between 1909–1969. Part I 1909–1929 National Omnibus & Transport Company (Oxford Publishing Co., 1979)
CRAWLEY, R. J., MACGREGOR, D. R. & SIMPSON, F. D. –
The Years Between 1909–1969. Part II The Eastern National Story From 1930 (Oxford Publishing Co., 1984)
GORDON, D. I. –
A Regional History Of The Railways Of Great Britain, Volume V The Eastern Counties (David & Charles, 1968)

ENTERTAINMENTS & SPORT

BUTLER, Nicholas – *Theatre In Colchester* (Nicholas Butler, 1981)
LEMMON, David and McCONNEL, Michael – *Essex County Cricket Club: The Official History* (Heinemann, 1987)
PEART, Stephen – *The Picture House In East Anglia* (Terence Dalton, 1980)

SCHOOLS & COLLEGES

REYNOLDS, Colin – *Illustrated History Of Wilson Marriage School* (Privately, 1984)

COLCHESTER ROYAL GRAMMAR SCHOOL

BARTON, B. A. B. (Ed) – *Seventy Years Of Schoolboy Memories* (The Old Colcestrian Society, 1972)
DAVIDSON, Paul and MACHELL, Dave (Ed) –
C.R.G.S. Quarter Centenary 1584-1984 – A Commemorative History (The Old Colcestrian Society, 1984)
JEFFREY, P. Shaw and BENHAM, Sir Gurney –
Some Chapters In The History Of The Royal Grammar School, Colchester (Benham and Company, 1948)